THE LEDWIDGE TREASURY

THE LEDWIDGE TREASURY
Selected Poems of
Francis Ledwidge
Edited by Dermot Bolger

Introduction by Seamus Heaney

Afterword by Dermot Bolger

**NEW
ISLAND**

The Ledwidge Treasury
First published 2007
by New Island
2 Brookside
Dundrum Road
Dublin 14

www.newisland.ie

The moral rights of the authors have been asserted.

ISBN   978 1 905494 56 9

British Library Cataloguing in Publication Data.
A CIP catalogue record for this book is available
from the British Library.

Typeset by TypeIT, Dublin
Cover design by Inka Hagen at New Island
Printed in Finland by WS Bookwell Ltd.

Contents

Editor's Note

Dermot Bolger

This volume has its origins in a lifelong ambition of mine to finally see into print a *Selected Poems* by Francis Ledwidge. This selection first appeared in 1992. It has been out of print for some time and is now being published with additional material to mark the 90th anniversary of the poet's death. In his own lifetime, Ledwidge only saw one small volume of his poetry in print and was awaiting the appearance of his second, *Songs of Peace,* when he was killed by a stray shell at Ypres on 31 July 1917, while – in a cruel irony – working at the same job he had spent so much of his early manhood in Meath doing – building a road through mud. *Songs of Peace*, which appeared three months later, was followed by *Last Songs*, edited, like the first two, by Lord Dunsany, and all three collections were quickly put together to form a *Complete Poems*, which went through a number of editions between then and 1955.

However, this *Complete Poems* left out a great deal of material. Alice Curtayne compiled a much extended *Complete Poems* in 1974, which served to reveal the full achievement of Francis Ledwidge as a poet. However, it forsook any chronological approach to the poems and instead grouped them under thematic headings like Birds and Blossoms, Flights of Fancy and Months and Seasons.

In making this selection of the best of his work, I have regrouped the poems back into their original three volumes and added in a number of poems uncovered by Alice Curtayne (marked by the initials C.P. for *Complete Poems*) where I feel they roughly belong in time. In *Songs of Peace*, either Ledwidge or Dunsany had grouped the poems according to where they were written and, where available, I have added these locations and dates in brackets.

INTRODUCTION

Seamus Heaney

It was appropriate that the excellent biography of Francis Ledwidge which appeared in 1972 should have been written by Alice Curtayne, a scholar noted more for her works on religious subjects than for her literary studies. Even though Ms Curtayne did once publish a study of Dante, her name, like Ledwidge's, evokes a certain nostalgia for those decades when this poet was appropriated and gratefully cherished as the guarantor of an Ireland domesticated, pious and demure; his poems used to be a safe bet for the convent library and the school prize, a charm against all that modernity which threatened the traditional values of a country battening down for independence. But Ledwidge's fate had been more complex and more modern than that. He very deliberately chose not to bury his head in local sand and, as a consequence, faced the choices and moral challenges of his times with solitude, honesty and rare courage. This integrity, and its ultimately gratifying effects upon his poetry, should command the renewed interest and respect of Irish people at the present time: Ledwidge lived through a similar period of historical transition when political, cultural and constitutional crises put into question values which had previously appeared as ratified and immutable as the contours of the land itself.

A lot of Irish people can still quote at least one line of his poetry. 'He shall not hear the bittern cry,' they say, and then memory falters until the final image of 'Thomas McDonagh' comes back, and they make a stab at something about the Dark Cow 'lifting her horn in pleasant meads'. For many of these people, Ledwidge vaguely belongs to the moment of

1916 and his note plays in with poems like Joseph Mary Plunkett's 'I see his blood upon the rose' and Padraig Pearse's 'Mise Eire', so that he is conceived of as somebody who 'sang to sweeten Ireland's wrong'. But for others, the abiding impression left by this poet is one of political ambivalence. For these people, the salient factor is his enlistment in the British Army in 1914 and his being in its ranks during the Easter Rising, in the uniform of those who executed, among others, Thomas McDonagh. The blame for this inconvenient *shoneenism,* however, is then laid at the aristocratic feet of Lord Dunsany, Ledwidge's most helpful mentor, literary agent and patron, so that in this scenario the poet shows up as a naïve patriot betrayed by the scheming Unionist peer into an act that went against his truest dispositions and convictions.

As Alice Curtayne's biography (to which I am here greatly indebted) makes clear, neither of these versions will do. To see him as the uncomplicated voice of romantic nationalism misrepresents the agonized consciousness which held in balance and ultimately decided between the command to act upon the dictates of a morality he took to be both objective and universally applicable, and the desire to keep faith with a politically resistant and particularly contentious Irish line. To see him as the dupe of a socially superior and politically insidious West British toff is to underrate his intelligence, his independence and the consciously fatal nature of his decision to enlist. For Ledwidge was no wilting flower; as James Stephens wrote of him:

I met him twice and then only for a few minutes. He is what we call here 'a lump of a lad' and he was panoplied in all the protective devices, or disguises, which a countryman puts on when he meets a man of the town!

This is the Ledwidge who is now commemorated by a plaque placed first on the bridge over the River Boyne at Slane, and then on the restored labourer's cottage outside the village where he was born on 19 August 1887, the second youngest in a surviving family of four brothers and three sisters. That the plaque appeared on the bridge first rather than the house has a certain appropriateness also, since the bridge, like the poet, was actually and symbolically placed between two Irelands.

Upstream, then and now, were situated several pleasant and potent reminders of an Anglicized, assimilated country: the Marquis of Conyngham's parkland sweeping down to the artfully wooded banks of the river, the waters of the river itself pouring their delicious sheen over the weir; Slane Castle and the big house at Beauparc; the canal and the towpath – here was an Irish landscape in which a young man like Ledwidge would be as likely to play cricket (he did) as Gaelic football (which he did also). The whole scene was as composed and historical as a topographical print, and possessed the tranquil allure of the established order of nine-teenth-century, post-union Ireland. Downstream, however, there were historical and prehistorical reminders of a different sort which operated as a strong counter-establish-ment influence in the young Ledwidge's mind. The Boyne battlefield, the megalithic tombs at Newgrange, Knowth and Dowth, the Celtic burying ground at Rosnaree – these things were beginning to be construed as part of the mystical body of an Irish culture which had suffered mutilation and was in need of restoration. Ledwidge would also have known about local associations with St Patrick, Cormac Mac Airt, Aengus the love god and many other legendary figures; and not far away was the Hill of Tara, where his mother filled his mind with the usual lore:

That old mill, built on the site of the first cornmill ever erected in Ireland, used to belong to my father's people when everybody had their own and these broad acres and leopard-coloured woods, almost as far as Kilcairne, all these were ours one time.

In a fairly obvious way then, the map of the field of Ledwidge's affections reflected the larger map of the conflicting cultural and political energies which were operative in Ireland throughout his lifetime. Furthermore, it could be argued that the weaker, nambier side of his poetry represents both a simplification of this divided predicament and a compensation for it. There is something regressive in the way he often seems to be holding on to the skirts of a maternal landscape. His melodiousness can at times verge upon the infantile and, indeed, a conventional Oedipal reading of Ledwidge's temperament makes a lot of sense. Not only did he project the mother into the scenes around him, but he was also conspicuously hampered in his relationships with the two young women he fell for. He was content enough romping round *ceilidhes* and football matches and *feiseanna* with other young men, indulging in the horseplay that never mutates into foreplay; he was popular, handsome and noticeable; long before it was fashionable, he wore a tweed suit, and once his first book of poems had been accepted for publication he affected a flowing Byronic necktie. But for all his dash, he was unforceful and sentimental when it came to his two romances, first with Ellie Vaughey, the daughter of a local farmer, and then Lizzie Healy, a sister of the schoolteacher in Slane. Deeply attached as he was to Ellie, he seems to have accepted their separation as inevitable when her parents insisted she stop seeing him because he was socially a cut beneath her. (She would marry a farmer called O'Neill.) And with Lizzie, a lot of time seems to have been spent in tiffs about a bunch of violets which he had sent her on Valentine's Day and a poem which he had not published in the *Meath Chronicle*. It is significant, indeed, that it was only after Ellie died that Ledwidge seems to have been emotionally and artistically capable of dealing with the experience by imagining her (typically) into flowers of the field.

Ledwidge did achieve a detached and tested selfhood, but not by the Joycean method of rejection. The pathos of a poem like 'My Mother' is a far cry from the imaginative detachment evident in the presentation of Mrs Dedalus in *Ulysses;* and yet the poem is not without its own touches of self-awareness. The lines about her 'earthly lover' who 'kissed away the music from her lips' nicely evoke the figure of the wife martyred to domestic life, enduring the death of personality in the birth of familial responsibility (Ledwidge's father died when he was four and the mother did constant housework and field work right up until the poet's early manhood). Furthermore, the poet's recognition of his own emotional timidities and capitulations are very wistfully rendered in the accurate if indulgent self-portrait with which the poem ends: 'This poor bird-hearted singer of a day'.

Ledwidge would not attain victory over the birdheartedness until the conflicting energies of his times and his temperament found themselves in alignment. Much in him that was ready to break out remained beyond the reach of his writing. He could bring the instinctive nostalgic Celtic side of Slane life to literary fruition in a poem like 'The Wife of Llew' but a gap remained between the genteel idiom which he understandably foisted on himself and the local life which he totally and unselfconsciously embodied. He might read Longfellow, have literary exchanges with the curate like one Father Smyth, discourse and share poems in manuscript with his fiddler friend, Matty McGoona, send work out to

The Drogheda Independent, but this side of his doings must have seemed disjunct from much else that was significant and central to his own and his generation's experience. The Keatsian idiom he inherited and Dunsany's ambitions for him as a writer had not much to do with his work as a road surfacerman, his work in the coppermines of Beauparc, his involvement with trade-union politics there and eventual dismissal for organising a strike against bad conditions; his fights at football matches in Navan; his participation in amateur dramatics; his activity as a member of Navan Rural Council, as a worker in an insurance office in that town and as secretary of the Irish Volunteers when they were eventually set up in Slane.

The character who was fit for all this was obviously much more robust than the writing in many of his poems would suggest. Not only did the salon idiom put him at some debilitated distance from himself, but the one tradition he naturally possessed – that of the local ballad of love and/or exile – was artistically too naïve to encompass the things that would happen to him. When Ledwidge was on board ship for Gallipoli, for example, he wrote 'Crockaharna', which represents this poet at his worst – even if it is a worst which is in an odd way authentic, all of a piece with recitations and party-pieces at *ceilidhe* houses like the McGoona's, continuous with the tenor on the stage at the variety concert.

Lord Dunsany, in fact, was not capable of bringing Ledwidge all that far beyond this. Obviously, he was practically extremely generous and well disposed, arranging for the publication of his books and writing introductions to them; but as a critic, he was capable of little beyond scolding his protégé for pretentious or archaic poeticisms. What he did do, however, was to introduce Ledwidge to his own Irish contemporaries in the craft, people such as

Thomas McDonagh, Padraic Colum, James Stephens, AE (George Russell) and Oliver St John Gogarty. These writers had ideas about the specific challenges and developments which were opening up for poetry in Ireland, and had produced work that gave credence to the idea that the creation of a distinctive Irish literature in English was under way. By putting Ledwidge in touch with them, Dunsany did open the doors of perception and self-awareness wider than the young poet might have managed on his own. Poems on mythological themes, very Yeatsian performances, admittedly began to appear and a finer, more objective way with verse-craft began to be in evidence (as in, for example, 'The Wife of Llew'). Yet for a long time, Ledwidge did not really have a compelling theme. According to W.B. Yeats's famous phrase, it is out of 'the quarrel with ourselves' that poetry comes, and it was only when this particular inner quarrel flared and could not be placated or resolved that Ledwidge's full force, as a personality, a poet and a morally sensitive creature, became engaged. This happened after John Redmond's epoch-making speech at Woodenbridge on 20 September 1913, a speech which split the Irish Volunteers and put a cruel strain on Ledwidge. He was, after all, an office bearer of the organisation at local level and imaginatively susceptible to the honourable motives behind both Redmond's breakaway National Volunteers (willing to be recruited to the British war effort) and the recalcitrant rump of the Irish Volunteers (who stuck to a more separatist reading of the Volunteers' original pledge 'to secure and maintain the rights and loyalties common to the whole people of Ireland'). The formation of the Irish Volunteers in the first place had been a direct response to the formation of the Ulster Volunteers, so even though the ideal they were meant to defend was Home Rule by Parliamentary process, they were still part of the surge towards Irish independence that had grown more definite in the years before 1914. Thus, when Redmond urged them 'to drill and make themselves efficient for the work ... not only in Ireland itself, but wherever the firing line extends in defence of rights of freedom and religion in this war', he was radically complicating the issue for everybody involved.

Ledwidge held out with the rump. At Navan Rural Council, on 10 October 1914, he would not be associated with a motion congratulating Redmond. Nine days later, he was the only member to hold out against the general agreement within the Rural Council to rescind its advertising contracts with *The Volunteer,* the organ of the pre-split movement, now continuing in rivalry to Redmond's paper, *The National Volunteer.* The prevailing mood of the movement was expressed in council by several of the members:

> Mr Bowens: *The young men of Meath would be better off fighting on the fields of France for the future of Ireland. That was his opinion, and he would remark that he was sorry to see there in the town of Navan – and probably in the village of Slane where Mr Ledwidge came from – ... a few Sinn Féiners that followed the tail end of MacNeill's party. There was nothing but strife in the country as long as these people had anything to do with the country ... What was England's uprise would be also Ireland's uprise.*
> (*Applause*)
> Mr Ledwidge: *England's uprise has always been Ireland's downfall.*
> Mr Owens: *... What was he (Mr Ledwidge)? Was he an Irishman or a pro-German?*
> Mr Ledwidge: *I am an anti-German and an Irishman.*

Five days after these exchanges, Francis Ledwidge enlisted in the Royal Inniskilling Fusiliers at Richmond Barracks. Some say because Ellie Vaughey was going to marry John O'Neill, which could have been part of the reason. Some say because Lord Dunsany coaxed him, which he almost certainly did not. I am tempted to say what Ledwidge himself said after the event:

> *I joined the British Army because she stood between Ireland and an enemy common to our civilization and I would not have her say that she defended us while we did nothing at home but pass resolutions.*
>
> *This is surely one of the rare occasions in English when an army is given the feminine gender, and it prompts one to speculate that Ledwidge's solidarity in the ranks was a further acting out of his identification with the hard years which his mother had done in the field on his behalf, an instance of compulsion to acknowledge such service with a corresponding gesture of self-sacrifice. At any rate, the statement makes it clear that Ledwidge acted with premeditation and out of a conflict of feelings. A sense of honour, a rage of exasperation, a preconscious compulsion: whatever the reason, it propelled him through the hell of campaigns on three fronts, first at Gallipoli, then in the Balkans and finally in the trenches and dug-outs of Ypres where he was killed by an exploding shell on 31 July 1917.*

Meanwhile, at Easter 1916, England's difficulty had been Ireland's opportunity. The rising occurred, the leaders were shot and the mood of the country began to change. As it did, Ledwidge's mood darkened also. On 20 April that year, on his way back to Ireland for a sick leave after a devastating retreat march to Salonika, Ledwidge could write to Dunsany:

Coming from Southhampton in the train, looking on England's beautiful valleys all white with spring, I thought indeed its freedom was worth all the blood I have seen flow. No wonder England has so many ardent patriots. I would be one of them myself did I not presume to be an Irish patriot.

A couple of weeks later, while he was convalescing in Slane, Ledwidge's equanimity would be shattered. In Richmond Barracks, where he enlisted, Thomas McDonagh and Joseph Mary Plunkett would be sentenced to death and then executed at Arbour Hill by soldiers in the uniform he had elected to wear as an act of Irish patriotism.

It is needless to elaborate on the pain of all this and not surprising to find him being court-martialled during this same leave for offensive remarks to a superior officer. He drank more than usual. He reported late for duty. But he did not desert. Instead, he wrote the poem by which he is best remembered, 'Thomas McDonagh', and harnessed his patriotic impulse to the task of sounding the Irish note which McDonagh himself had discovered in Irish poetry and had to some extent prescribed for it. His new command of the Gaelic techniques of assonance and internal rhyme constituted an oblique declaration of loyalty to a complex of feelings not represented by the uniform in which he fought. Ledwidge would go on to write other poems in the aftermath of 1916, all of them showing more point and bite than his early nature lyrics but none of them as perfect a realisation of his gifts as this one. It is a poem in which his displaced hankering for the place beyond confusion and his own peculiar melancholy voice find a subject which exercises them entirely, no doubt because in lamenting McDonagh he was to a large extent lamenting himself:

He shall not hear the bittern cry
In the wild sky, where he is lain,
Nor voices of the sweeter birds
Above the wailing of the rain.

Nor shall he know when loud March blows
Thro' slanting snows her fanfare shrill,
Blowing to flame the golden cup
Of many an upset daffodil.

But when the Dark Cow leaves the moor,
And pastures poor with greedy weeds,
Perhaps he'll hear her low at morn
Lifting her horn in pleasant meads.

Ledwidge solved nothing. As a poet, his sense of purpose and his own gifts were only beginning to come into mature focus. As a political phenomenon, he represents conflicting elements in the Irish inheritance which continue to be repressed or unresolved. There is still minimal public acknowledgement in Ireland of the part played by Irish soldiers in the First World War, although their devotion to the ideal of independence was passionate in its day; and we do now see the development of a corresponding unwillingness to acknowledge the heroic aspect of the 1916 Rising. Perhaps, too, the meaning of his choice has lost resonance because the concept of personal integrity as a relevant factor in political decision has been gradually eroding: a Marxist-influenced consensus tends to put the onus on the individual to make a correct theoretical assessment of what is historically progressive rather than act upon some internalised moral principle. Nevertheless, the combination of vulnerability and adequacy which Ledwidge displayed in facing the life of his times remains admirable and as people in Ireland today prepare to encounter the dilemmas of their own times – moral, constitutional, domestic, international – his example constitutes a challenge to act with solitary resolve and to expect neither consensus nor certitude.

In the literary reckoning, Yeats's Irish airman foreseeing his death with an absolved exhilaration – 'A lonely impulse of delight/Led to this tumult in the clouds' – may manifest both the triumph and the immunity of greater artistic genius: in such company, Ledwidge is neither a very strong nor a very original talent. Yet this 'bird-hearted singer' keeps the nest warm and the lines open for a different poetry, one that might combine tendermindedness towards the predicaments of others with an ethically unsparing attitude towards the self. Indeed, it is because of this scruple, this incapacity for grand and overbearing certainties, and not because of the uniform he wore, it is for this reason that Ledwidge can be counted as a 'war poet' in the company of Wilfred Owen and Siegfried Sassoon. Yet his status as a combatant is finally not as important as his membership of the company of the walking wounded, wherever they are to be found at any given time.

In Memoriam Francis Ledwidge

Killed in France 31 July 1917

The bronze soldier hitches a bronze cape
That crumples stiffly in imagined wind
No matter how the real winds buff and sweep
His sudden hunkering run, forever craned

Over Flanders. Helmet and haversack,
The gun's firm slope from butt to bayonet,
The loyal, fallen names on the embossed plaque –
It all meant little to the worried pet.

I was in nineteen forty-six or seven,
Gripping my Aunt Mary by the hand
Along the Portstewart prom, then round the crescent
To thread the Castle Walk out to the strand.

The pilot from Coleraine sailed to the coal-boat.
Courting couples rose out of the scooped dunes.
A farmer stripped to his studs and shiny waistcoat
Rolled the trousers down on his timid shins.

Francis Ledwidge, you courted at the seaside
Beyond Drogheda one Sunday afternoon.
Literary, sweet-talking, countrified,
You pedalled out the leafy road from Slane

Where you belonged, among the dolorous
And lovely: the May altar of wild flowers,
Easter water sprinkled in outhouses,
Mass-rocks and hill-top raths and raftered byres.

I think of you in your Tommy's uniform,
A haunted Catholic face, pallid and brave,
Ghosting the trenches like a bloom of hawthorn
Or silence cored from a Boyne passage-grave.

It's summer, nineteen-fifteen. I see the girl
My aunt was then, herding on the long acre.
Behind a low bush in the Dardanelles
You suck stones to make your dry mouth water.

It's nineteen-seventeen. She still herds cows
But a big strafe puts the candles out in Ypres:
'My soul is by the Boyne, cutting new meadows...
My country wears her confirmation dress.'

'To be called a British soldier while my country
Has no place among nations...' You were rent
By shrapnel six weeks later. 'I am sorry
That party politics should divide our tents.'

In you, our dead enigma, all the strains
Criss-cross in useless equilibrium
And as the wind tunes through this vigilant bronze
I hear again the sure confusing drum

You followed from Boyne water to the Balkans
But miss the twilit note your flute should sound.
You were not keyed or pitched like these true-blue ones
Though all of you consort now underground.

Seamus Heaney

A Little Boy in the Morning

He will not come, and still I wait.
He whistles at another gate
Where angels listen. Ah, I know
He will not come, yet if I go
How shall I know he did not pass
Barefooted in the flowery grass?

The moon leans on one silver horn
Above the silhouettes of morn,
And from their nest-sills finches whistle
Or stooping pluck the downy thistle.
How is the morn so gay and fair
Without his whistling in its air?

The world is calling, I must go.
How shall I know he did not pass
Barefooted in the shining grass?

S. O. P.
(At Home)

Songs of the Fields
(1915)

Behind the Closed Eye

I walk the old frequented ways
That wind around the tangled braes,
I live again the sunny days
Ere I the city knew.

And scenes of old again are born,
The woodbine lassoing the thorn,
And drooping Ruth-like in the corn
The poppies weep the dew.

Above me in their hundred schools
The magpies bend their young to rules,
And like an apron full of jewels
The dewy cobweb swings.

And frisking in the stream below
The troutlets make the circles flow,
And the hungry crane doth watch them grow
As a smoker does his rings.

Above me smokes the little town,
With its whitewashed walls and roofs of brown
And its octagon spire toned smoothly down
As the holy minds within.

And wondrous impudently sweet,
Half of him passion, half conceit,
The blackbird calls adown the street
Like the piper of Hamelin.

I hear him, and I feel the lure
Drawing me back to the homely moor,
I'll go and close the mountains' door
On the city's strife and din.

(1902)

Within the oak a throb of pigeon wings
Fell silent, and grey twilight hushed the fold,
And spiders' hammocks swung on half-oped things
That shook like foreigners upon our cold.
A gipsy lit a fire and made a sound
Of moving tins, and from an oblong moon
The river seemed to gush across the ground
To the cracked metre of a marching tune.

And then three syllables of melody
Dropped from a blackbird's flute, and died apart
Far in the dewy dark. No more but three,
Yet sweeter music never touched a heart
'Neath the blue domes of London. Flute and reed,
Suggesting feelings of the solitude
When will was all the Delphi I would heed,
Lost like a wind within a summer wood
From little knowledge where great sorrows brood.

(1914)

DESIRE IN SPRING

I love the cradle songs that mothers sing
In lonely places when the twilight drops,
The slow endearing melodies that bring
Sleep to the weeping lids; and, when she stops,
I love the roadside birds upon the tops
Of dusty hedges in a world of Spring.

And when the sunny rain drips from the edge
Of midday wind, and meadows lean one way,
And a long whisper passes thro' the sedge,
Beside the broken water let me stay,
While these old airs upon my memory play,
And silent changes colour up the hedge.

(1914)

MAY MORNING

Young May came peeping o'er the mount
And dressed herself before the font.
The glow-worm snuffed his candle bright.
The brooklet tumbled into light.
The skylark sang into the blue.
The baby corn sprang into view.
The merle piped beside the rill.
The mavis answered from the hill
The daisy crowned each grassy bleb.
The spider crossed his dewy web.
The wood-pecker the hazel tapped
And straight its little leaves unwrapped.
The snipe forsook his marshy bed.
The ceannabawn raised up its head
And still the harper played away
The march of morning into day.

C.P.
(Drogheda Independent, 1912)

24

JUNE

Broom out the floor now, lay the fender by,
And plant this bee-sucked bough of woodbine there,
And let the window down. The butterfly
Floats in upon the sunbeam, and the fair
Tanned face of June, the nomad gipsy, laughs
Above her widespread wares, the while she tells
The farmers' fortunes in the fields, and quaffs
The water from the spider-peopled wells.

The hedges are all drowned in green grass seas,
And bobbing poppies flare like Elmo's light,
While siren-like the pollen-stained bees
Drone in the clover depths. And up the height
The cuckoo's voice is hoarse and broke with joy.
And on the lowland crops the crows make raid,
Nor fear the clappers of the farmer's boy,
Who sleeps, like drunken Noah, in the shade.

And loop this red rose in that hazel ring
That snares your little ear, for June is short
And we must joy in it and dance and sing,
And from her bounty draw her rosy worth.
Ay! soon the swallows will be flying south,
The wind wheel north to gather in the snow,
Even the roses spilt on youth's red mouth
Will soon blow down the road all roses go.

AUGUST

She'll come at dusky first of day,
White over yellow harvest's song.
Upon her dewy rainbow way
She shall be beautiful and strong.
The lidless eye of noon shall spray
Tan on her ankles in the hay,
Shall kiss her brown the whole day long.

I'll know her in the windows, tall
Above the crickets of the hay.
I'll know her when her odd eyes fall,
One May-blue, one November-grey.
I'll watch her down the red barn wall
Take down her rusty scythe, and call,
And I will follow her away.

THE HILLS

The hills are crying from the fields to me,
And calling me with music from a choir
Of waters in their woods where I can see
The bloom unfolded on the whins like fire.
And, as the evening moon climbs ever higher
And blots away the shadows from the slope,
They cry to me like things devoid of hope.

The Pigeons are home. Day droops. The fields are cold.
Now a slow wind comes labouring up the sky.
With a small cloud long steeped in sunset gold,
Like Jason with the precious fleece anigh
The harbour of Iolcos. Day's bright eye
Is filmed with the twilight, and the rill
Shines like a scimitar upon the hill.

And moonbeams drooping thro' the coloured wood
Are full of little people winged white.
I'll wander thro' the moon-pale solitude
That calls across the intervening night
With river voices at their utmost height,
Sweet as rain-water in the blackbird's flute
That strikes the world in admiration mute.

The Wife of Llew

And Gwydion said to Math, when it was Spring:
'Come now and let us make a wife for Llew.'
And so they broke broad boughs yet moist with dew,
And in a shadow made a magic ring:
They took the violet and the meadowsweet
To form her pretty face, and for her feet
They built a mound of daisies on a wing,
And for her voice they made a linnet sing
In the wide poppy blowing for her mouth.
And over all they chanted twenty hours.
And Llew came singing from the azure south
And bore away his wife of birds and flowers.

To a Linnet in a Cage

When Spring is in the fields that stained your wing,
And the blue distance is alive with song,
And finny quiets of the gabbling spring
Rock lilies red and long,
At dewy daybreak, I will set you free
In ferny turnings of the woodbine lane,
Where faint-voiced echoes leave and cross in glee
The hilly swollen plain.

In draughty houses you forget your tune,
The modulator of the changing hours.
You want the wide air of the moody noon,
And the slanting evening showers.
So I will loose you, and your song shall fall
When morn is white upon the dewy pane,
Across my eyelids, and my soul recall
From worlds of sleeping pain.

THOUGHTS AT THE TRYSTING STILE

Come, May, and hang a white flag on each thorn,
Make truce with earth and heaven; the April child
Now hides her sulky face deep in the morn
Of your new flowers by the water wild
And in the ripples of the rising grass,
And rushes bent to let the south wind pass
On with her tumult of swift nomad wings,
And broken domes of downy dandelion.
Only in spasms now the blackbird sings.
The hour is all a-dream.
Nets of woodbine
Throw woven shadows over dreaming flowers,
And dreaming, a bee-luring lily bends
Its tender bell where blue dyke-water cowers
Thro' briars and folded ferns, and gripping ends
Of wild convolvulus.

The lark's sky-way
Is desolate.
I watch an apple-spray
Beckon across a wall as if it knew
I wait the calling of the orchard maid.
Inly I feel that she will come in blue,
With yellow on her hair, and two curls strayed
Out of her comb's loose stocks, and I shall steal
Behind and lay my hands upon her eyes,
'Look not, but be my Psyche!'
And her peal
laughter will ring far, and as she tries
For freedom I will call her names of flowers
That climb up walls; then thro' the twilight hours

We'll talk about the loves of ancient queens,
And kisses like wasp-honey, false and sweet,
And how we are entangled in love's snares
Like wind-looped flowers
Like wind-looped flowers.

Before the Tears

You looked as sad as an eclipsed moon
Above the sheaves of harvest, and there lay
A light lisp on your tongue, and very soon
The petals of your deep blush fell away;
White smiles that come with an uneasy grace
From inner sorrow crossed your forehead fair,
When the wind passing took your scattered hair
And flung it like a brown shower in my face.

Tear-fringed winds that fill the heart's low sighs
And never break upon the bosom's pain,
But blow unto the windows of the eyes
Their misty promises of silver rain,
Around your loud heart ever rose and fell.
I thought 'twere better that the tears should come
And strike your every feeling wholly numb,
o thrust my hand in yours and shook farewell.

All-Hallows Eve

The dreadful hour is sighing for a moon
To light old lovers to the place of tryst,
And old footsteps from blessed acres soon
On old known pathways will be lightly prest;
And winds that went to eavesdrop since the noon,
Kinking at some old tale told sweetly brief,
Will give a cowslick to the yarrow leaf,
And sling the round nut from the hazel down.

And there will be old yarn-balls, and old spells
In broken lime-kilns, and old eyes will peer
For constant lovers in old spidery wells,
And old embraces will grow newly dear,
And some may meet old lovers in old dells.
And some in doors ajar in towns light-lorn;
But two will meet beneath a gnarly thorn
Deep in the bosom of the windy fells.

Then when the night slopes home and white-faced day
Yawns in the east there will be sad farewells;
And many feet will tap a lonely way
Back to the comfort of their chilly cells,
And eyes will backward turn and long to stay
Where love first found them in the clover bloom –
But one will never seek the lonely tomb,
And two will linger at the tryst alway.

A Fear

I roamed the woods to-day and seemed to hear,
As Dante heard, the voice of suffering trees.
The twisted roots seemed bare contorted knees,
The bark was full of faces strange with fear.

I hurried home still wrapt in that dark spell,
And all the night upon the world's great lie
I pondered, and a voice seemed whisp'ring high,
'You died long since, and all this thing is hell!'

Before the War of Cooley

At daybreak Maeve rose up from where she prayed
And took her prophetess across her door
To gaze upon her hosts. Tall spear and blade
Burnished for early battle dimly shook
The morning's colours, and then Maeve said:
'Look
And tell me how you see them now.'

And then
The woman that was lean with knowledge said:
'There's crimson on them, and there's dripping red.'
And a tall soldier galloped up the glen
With foam upon his boot, and halted there
Beside old Maeve. She said, 'Not yet,' and turned
Into her blazing dun, and knelt in prayer
One solemn hour, and once again she came
And sought her prophetess. With voice that mourned
'How do you see them now?' she asked.
'All lame
And broken in the noon.' And once again
The soldier stood before her.

'No, not yet'
Maeve answered his inquiring look and turned
Once more unto her prayer, and yet once more
'How do you see them now?' she asked.
'All wet
With storm rains, and all broken, and all tore
With midnight wolves.' And when the soldier came
Maeve said, 'It is the hour.' There was a flash
Of trumpets in the dim, a silver flame

Of rising shields, loud words passed down the ranks,
And twenty feet they saw the lances leap.
They passed the dun with one short noisy dash.
And turning proud Maeve gave the wise one thanks,
And sought her chamber in the dun to weep.

GOD'S REMEMBRANCE

There came a whisper from the night to me
Like music of the sea, a mighty breath
From out the valley's dewy mouth, and Death
Shook his lean bones, and every coloured tree
Wept in the fog of morning. From the town
Of nests among the branches one old crow
With gaps upon his wings flew far away.
And, thinking of the golden summer glow,
I heard a blackbird whistle half his lay
Among the spinning leaves that slanted down.

And I who am a thought of God's now long
Forgotten in His Mind, and desolate
With other dreams long over, as a gate
Singing upon the wind the anvil song,
Sang of the Spring when first he dreamt of me
In that old town all hills and signs that creak:
And He remembered me as something far
In old imaginations, something weak
With distance, like a little sparkling star
Drowned in the lavender of evening sea.

THE VISION ON THE BRINK

To-night when you sit in the deep hours alone,
And from the sleeps you snatch wake quick and feel
You hear my step upon the threshold-stone,
My hand upon the doorway latchward steal,
Be sure 'tis but the white winds of the snow,
For I shall come no more.

And when the candle in the pane is wore,
And moonbeams down the hill long shadows throw,
When night's white eyes are in the chinky door,
Think of a long road in a valley low,
Think of a wanderer in the distance far,
Lost like a voice among the scattered hills.

And when the moon has gone and oceans spills
Its waters backward from the trysting bar,
And in dark furrows of the night there tills
A jewelled plough, and many a falling star
Moves you to prayer, then will you think of me
On the long road that will not ever end.

Jonah his hoarse in Nineveh – I'd lend
My voice to save the town – and hurriedly
Goes Abraham with murdering knife, and Ruth
Is weary in the corn... Yet will I stay,
For one flower blooms upon the rocks of truth,
God is in all our hurry and delay.

WAITING

A strange old woman on the wayside sate,
Looking far away and shook her head and sighed.
And when anon, close by, a rusty gate,
Loud on the warm winds cried,
She lifted up her eyes and said, 'You're late.'
Then shook her head and sighed.

And evening found her thus, and night in state
Walked thro' the starlight, and a heavy tide
Followed the yellow moon around her to wait,
And morning walked in wide.
She lifted up her eyes and said, 'You're late.'
Then shook her head and sighed.

SONGS OF PEACE
(1917)

THE PLACE

Blossoms as old as May I scatter here,
And a blue wave I lifted from the stream.
It shall not know when winter days are drear
Or March is hoarse with blowing. But a-dream
The laurel boughs shall hold a canopy
Peacefully over it the winter long,
Till all the birds are back from oversea,
And April rainbows win a blackbird's song.

And when the war is over I shall take
My lute a-down to it and sing again
Songs of the whispering things amongst the brake,
And those I love shall know them by their strain.
Their airs shall be the blackbird's twilight song,
Their words shall be all flowers with fresh dews hoar.
But it is lonely now in winter long,
And, God! to hear the blackbird sing once more.

(In Barracks)

42

MAY

She leans across an orchard gate somewhere,
Bending from out the shadows to the light,
A dappled spray of blossom in her hair
Studded with dew-drops lovely from the night
She smiles to think how many hearts she'll smite
With beauty ere her robes fade from the lawn,
She hears the robin's cymbals with delight,
The skylarks in the rosebush of the dawn.

For her the cowslip rings its yellow bell,
For her the violets watch with wide blue eyes.
The wandering cuckoo doth its clear name tell
Thro' the white mist of blossoms where she lies
Painting a sunset for the western skies.
You'd know by her smile and by her tear
And by the way the swift and martin flies,
Where she is south of these wild days and drear.

(In Barracks)

TO EILISH OF THE FAIR HAIR

I'd make my heart a harp to play for you
Love songs within the evening dim of day,
Were it not dumb with ache and with mildew
Of sorrow withered like a flower away,
It hears so many calls from homeland places,
So many sighs from all it will remember,
From the pale roads and woodlands where your face is
Like laughing sunlight running thro' December.

But this it singeth loud above its pain,
To bring the greater ache: whate'er befall
The love that oft-times woke the sweeter strain
Shall turn to you always. And should you call
To pity it some day in those old places
Angels will covet the loud joy that fills it.
But thinking of the by-ways where your face is
Sunlight on other hearts – Ah! how it kills it.

(In Barracks)

44

THE GARDENER

Among the flowers, like flowers, her slow hands move
Easing a muffled bell or stooping low
To help sweet roses climb the stakes above,
Where pansies stare and seem to whisper 'Lo!'
Like gaudy butterflies her sweet peas blow
Filling the garden with dim rustlings. Clear
On the sweet Book she reads how long ago
There was a garden to a woman dear.

She makes her life one grand beatitude
Of Love and Peace, and with contented eyes
She sees not in the whole world mean or rude,
And her small lot she trebly multiplies.
And when the darkness muffles up the skies
Still to be happy is her sole desire,
She sings sweet songs about a great emprise,
And sees a garden blowing in the fire.

(At Sea)

LULLABY

Shall I take the rainbow out of the sky
And the moon from the well in the lane,
And break them in pieces to coax your eye
To slumber a wee while again?
Rock goes the cradle, and rock, and rock.
The mouse has stopped nibbling under the clock
And the crows have gone home to Slane.

The little lambs came from the hills of brown,
With pillows of wool for your fair little head.
And the birds from the bushes flew in with down
To make you snug in your cradle bed.
Rock goes the cradle, and rock, and rock.
The mouse has stopped nibbling under the clock.
And the birds and the lambs have fled.

There is wind from the bog. It will blow all night,
Upsetting the willows and scattering rain.
The poor little lambs will be crying with fright
For the kind little birds in the hedge of the lane.
Rock goes the cradle, and rock, and rock.
Sleep, little one, sleep, and the wet wind mock,
Till the crows come home from Slane.

C.P.
(1915)

46

THE HOME-COMING OF THE SHEEP

The sheep are coming home in Greece,
Hark the bells on every hill!
Flock by flock, and fleece by fleece,
Wandering wide a little piece
Thro' the evening red and still,
Stopping where the pathways cease,
Cropping with a hurried will.

Thro' the cotton-bushes low
Merry the boys with shouldered crooks
Close them in a single row,
Shout among them as they go
With one bell-ring o'er the brooks.
Such delight you never know
Reading it from gilded books.

Before the early stars are bright
Cormorants and sea-gulls call,
And the moon comes large and white
Filling with a lovely light
The ferny curtained waterfall.
Then sleep wraps every bell up tight
And the climbing moon grows small.

(In Greece)

MY MOTHER

God made my mother on an April day,
From sorrow and the mist along the sea,
Lost birds' and wanderers' songs and ocean spray,
And the moon loved her wandering jealously.

Beside the ocean's din she combed her hair,
Singing the nocturne of the passing ships,
Before her earthly lover found her there
And kissed away the music from her lips.

She came unto the hills and saw the change
That brings the swallow and the geese in turns.
But there was not a grief she deemed strange,
For there is that in her which always mourns.

Kind heart she has for all on hill or wave
Whose hopes grew wings like ants to fly away.
I bless the God Who such a mother gave
This poor bird-hearted singer of a day.

(In Hospital in Egypt)

TO ONE DEAD

A blackbird singing
On a moss-upholstered stone,
Bluebells swinging,
Shadows wildly blown,
A song in the wood,
A ship on the sea.
The song was for you
and the ship was for me.

A blackbird singing
I hear in my troubled mind,
Bluebells swinging
I see in a distant wind.
But sorrow and silence
Are the wood's threnody,
The silence for you
And the sorrow for me.

(In Hospital in Egypt)

SKREEN CROSS ROADS

Five roads meet on the hill of Skreen,
Five fair ways to wander down.
One road sings of the valleys green
Two of the Sea, and one of the town.
And one little road has never a song
Tho' the world be fair and the day be long.

This is the song the south road sings:
'I go where Love and Peace abide.
I pass the world's seven wondrous things
And cities fallen in their pride.
Sunny are the miles thro' which I stray
From the Southern Cross to the Milky Way.'

But for all its song is so sweet to hear
It has no melody for my ear.

This is the song the sea road sings:
'When the moon is full the tide is high;
And the little ships in the harbours swing
When the sea-birds tell that a storm is nigh,
And "Heave" the sailor calls, and "Ho!"
It is far to my love when the strong winds blow.'

Oh the lure of the roads that sing of the sea
Make my heart beat fast 'till it broke in me.

This is the song of the road to the town:
'Row by row stand the silent lights,
And the music of bells goes up and down
The slopes of the wind, and high delights
Lure in the folk from the valley farms.
It pulls down the hills with its great grey arms.'

It sings its song so low and sweet
That once or twice it has lured my feet.

But the dumb little road that winds to the north
Is the dearest road in the world to me.
I would give my soul – for what it is worth –
To be there in its silent company,
Telling it over my hopes and fears,
With only its silence consoling my ears.

C.P.
(In Hospital in Egypt, 3 April 1916)

Thomas McDonagh

He shall not hear the bittern cry
In the wild sky, where he is lain,
Nor voices of the sweeter birds
Above the wailing of the rain.

Nor shall he know when loud March blows
Thro' slanting snows her fanfare shrill,
Blowing to flame the golden cup
Of many an upset daffodil.

But when the Dark Cow leaves the moor,
And pastures poor with greedy weeds,
Perhaps he'll hear her low at morn
Lifting her horn in pleasant meads.

(In Barracks)

THE BLACKBIRDS

I heard the Poor Old Woman say:
'At break of day the fowler came,
And took my blackbirds from their songs
Who loved me well thro' shame and blame.

No more from lovely distances
Their songs shall bless me mile by mile,
Nor to white Ashbourne call me down
To wear my crown another while.

When bended flowers the angels mark
For the skylark the place they lie,
From there its little family
Shall dip their wings first in the sky.

And when the first surprise of flight
Sweet songs excite, from the far dawn
Shall there come blackbirds loud with love,
Sweet echoes of the singers gone.

But in the lonely hush of eve
Weeping I grieve the silent bills.'
I heard the Poor Old Woman say
In Derry of the little hills.

(In Barracks)

FATE

Lugh made a stir in the air
With his sword of cries,
And fairies thro' hidden ways
Came from the skies,
And their spells withered up the fair
And vanquished the wise.

And old lame Balor came down
With his gorgon eye
Hidden behind its lid,
Old, withered and dry.
He looked on the wattle town,
And the town passed by.

These things I know in my dreams,
The crying sword of Lugh,
And Balor's ancient eye
Searching me through,
Withering up my songs
And my pipe yet new.

(In Barracks)

At Currabwee

Every night at Currabwee
Little men with leather hats
Mend the boots of Faery
From the tough wings of the bats.
So my mother told to me,
And she is wise you will agree.

Louder than a cricket's wing
All night long their hammer's glee
Times the merry songs they sing
Of Ireland glorious and free.
So I heard Joseph Plunkett say,
You know he heard them but last May.

And when the night is very cold
They warm their hands against the light
Of stars that make the waters gold
Where they are labouring all the night.
So Pearse said, and he knew the truth,
Among the stars he spent his youth.

And I, myself, have often heard
Their singing as the stars went by,
For am I not of those who reared
The banner of old Ireland high,
From Dublin town to Turkey's shores,
And where the Vardar loudly roars?

C.P.

LAST SONGS
(1918)

AT EVENING

A broad field at a wood's high end,
Daylight out and the stars half lit,
And let the dark-winged bat go flit
About the river's wide blue bend.
But thoughts of someone once a friend
Shall be calling loud thro' the hills of Time.

Wide is the back-door of the Past
And I shall be leaving the slated town.
But no, the rain will be slanting brown
And large drops chasing the small ones fast
Down the wide pane, for a cloud was cast
On youth when he started the world to climb.

There won't be song, for song has died.
There won't be flowers for the flowers are done.
I shall see the red of a large cold sun
Wash down on the slow blue tide,
Where the noiseless deep fish glide,
In the dark wet shade of the heavy lime.

C.P.

To a Sparrow

Because you have no fear to mingle
Wings with those of greater part,
So like me, with song I single
Your sweet impudence of heart.

And when prouder feathers go where
Summer holds her leafy show,
You still come to us from nowhere
Like grey leaves across the snow.

In back ways where odd and end go
To your meals you drop down sure,
Knowing every broken window
Of the hospitable poor.

There is no bird half so harmless,
None so sweetly rude as you,
None so common and so charmless,
None of virtues nude as you.

But for all your faults I love you,
For you linger with us still,
Though the wintry winds reprove you
And the snow is on the hill.

HAD I A GOLDEN POUND
(After the Irish)

Had I a golden pound to spend,
My love should mend and sew no more.
And I would buy her a little quern,
Easy to turn on the kitchen floor.

And for her windows curtains white,
With birds in flight and flowers in bloom,
To face with pride the road to town,
And mellow down her sunlit room.

And with the silver change we'd prove
The truth of Love to life's own end,
With hearts the years could but embolden,
Had I a golden pound to spend.

After Court Martial

My mind is not my mind, therefore
I take no heed of what men say,
I lived ten thousand years before
God cursed the town of Nineveh.

The Present is a dream I see
Of horror and loud sufferings,
At dawn a bird will waken me
Unto my place among the kings.

And though men called me a vile name,
And all my dream companions gone,
'Tis I the solider bears the shame,
Not I the king of Babylon.

The Cobbler of Sari Gueul

A cobbler lives in Sari Gueul
Who has a wise mind, people say.
He sits in his door on a three-legged stool,
Hammering leather all the day.
He laughs with the boys who make such noise
And loves to watch how the children play.
Gladly I'd shuffle my lot in a pool
With that of the cobbler of Sari Gueul.

Sorrow to him is a ball of wax
That melts in the sun of a cheerful smile
And all his needs are, a box of tacks,
Thread and leather, old boots in a pile.
I would give my art for half of his heart.
Who wants the world with all its guile?
And which of us two is the greater fool,
Me, or the cobbler of Sari Gueul?

At evening an old cow climbs the street,
So lean and bony you'd wonder how.
He hears the old cracked bell from his seat
And the wrinkles move on his yellow brow,
And he says as he strikes, 'To me or my likes
You are coming faster, old brown cow.
Slow steps come fast to the knife and rule.'
Says the wise old cobbler of Sari Gueul.

Often I hear him in my sleep,
Hammering still in the little town.
And I see the queer old shops on the steep,
And the queerer folk move up and down.
And the cobbler's sign creaks up in a vine,
When the wind slips over the housetops brown.
Waking, I pray to the Gods who rule
For the queer old cobbler of Sari Gueul.

C.P.

Home

A burst of sudden wings at dawn,
Faint voices in a dreamy noon,
Evenings of mist and murmurings,
And nights with rainbows of the moon.

And through these things a wood-way dim,
And waters dim, and slow sheep seen
On uphill paths that wind away
Through summer sounds and harvest green.

This is a song a robin sang
This morning on a broken tree,
It was about the little fields
That call across the world to me.

The Dead Kings

All the dead kings came to me
At Rosnaree, where I was dreaming,
A few stars glimmered through the morn,
And down the thorn the dews were streaming.

And every dead king had a story
Of ancient glory, sweetly told.
It was too early for the lark,
But the starry dark had tints of gold.

I listened to the sorrows three
Of that Eire passed into song.
A cock crowed near a hazel croft,
And up aloft dim larks winged strong.

And I, too, told the kings a story
Of later glory, her fourth sorrow:
There was a sound like moving shields
In high green fields and the lowland furrow.

And one said: 'We who yet are kings
Have heard these things lamenting inly.'
Sweet music flowed from many a bill
And on the hill the morn stood queenly.

And one said: 'Over is the singing,
And bell bough ringing, whence we come;
With heavy hearts we'll tread the shadows,
In honey meadows birds are dumb.'

And one said: 'Since the poets perished
And all they cherished in the way,
Their thoughts unsung, like petal showers
Inflame the hours of blue and grey.'

And one said: 'A loud tramp of men
We'll hear once again at Rosnaree.'
A bomb burst near me where I lay.
I woke, 'twas day in Picardy.

TO ONE WHO COMES NOW AND THEN

When you come in, it seems a brighter fire
Crackles upon the hearth invitingly,
The household routine which was wont to tire
Grows full of novelty.

You sit upon our home-upholstered chair
And talk of matters wonderful and strange,
Of books, and travel, customs old which dare
The gods of Time and Change.

Till we with inner word our care refute
Laughing that this our bosoms yet assails,
While there are maidens dancing to a flute
In Andalusian vales.

And sometimes from my shelf of poems you take
And secret meanings to our hearts disclose,
As when the winds of June the mid bush shake
We see the hidden rose.

And when the shadows muster, and each tree
A moment flutters, full of shutting wings,
You take the fiddle and mysteriously
Wake wonders on the strings.

And in my garden, grey with misty flowers,
Low echoes fainter than a beetle's horn
Fill all the corners with it, like sweet showers
Of bells, in the owl's morn.

Come often, friend; with welcome and surprise
We'll greet you from the sea or from the town;
Come when you like and from whatever skies
Above you smile or frown.

(Belgium, 22 July 1917)

SOLILOQUY

When I was young I had a care
Lest I should cheat me of my share
Of that which makes it sweet to strive
For life, and dying still survive,
A name in sunshine written higher
Than lark or poet dare aspire.

But I grew weary doing well;
Besides, 'twas sweeter in that hell,
Down with the loud banditti people
Who robbed the orchards, climbed the steeple
For jackdaw's eggs and made the cock
Crow ere 'twas daylight on the clock.
I was so very bad the neighbours
Spoke of me at their daily labours.
And now I'm drinking wine in France
The helpless child of circumstance.
To-morrow will be loud with war,
How will I be accounted for?

It is too late now to retrieve
A fallen dream, too late to grieve
A name unmade, but not too late
To thank the gods for what is great;
A keen-edged sword, a soldier's heart,
Is greater than a poet's art.
And greater than a poet's fame
A little grave that has no name,
Whence honour turns away in shame.

With Flowers

These have more language than my song,
Take them and let them speak for me.
I whispered them a secret thing
Down the green lanes of Allary.

You shall remember quiet ways
Watching them fade, and quiet eyes,
And two hearts given up to love,
A foolish and an overwise.

A Soldier's Grave

Then in the lull of midnight, gentle arms
Lifted him slowly down the slopes of death,
Lest he should hear again the mad alarms
Of battle, dying moans, and painful breath.

And where the earth was soft for flowers we made
A grave for him that he might better rest.
So, Spring shall come and leave it sweet arrayed,
And there the lark shall turn her dewy nest.

MILESTONE TO MONUMENT:

A PERSONAL JOURNEY IN SEARCH OF FRANCIS LEDWIDGE

Dermot Bolger

For Donal Haughey

At the most unlikely times I think of the Irish poet, Francis Ledwidge. Maybe when playing tennis with my sons in a Dublin park or driving home late at night, opening my hall door, knowing that my wife is asleep upstairs. These simple acts were these futures that he missed, these mundane yet magical realities that he might have expected to know. Most Fridays I still play football on astro-turf near Dublin Airport. My ankles and back are gone but I pretend to cheat time a little longer because I want to prolong this brief plateau when my sons and I can share the one pitch.

Occasionally, I look beyond the floodlights at the planes landing and think of Ledwidge. He never knew a son or a wife for that matter. He never felt the need to cheat time, because time cheated him. Fate tackled him from behind, just a few weeks shy of his thirtieth birthday, when he was blown to pieces in Flanders by a stray shell during a lull in the first day of the nightmare Third Battle of Ypres. Whatever shattered parts of his limbs that could be gathered up were dumped in the crater left by that shell before the work of road building recommenced. His face became trapped inside a handful of photographs. He looks out at me from those old photos still, trapped in an innocence that he longed to shed, condemned to the limbo of being forever young.

However, like thousands of fellow Irishmen, Ledwidge was also condemned to another kind of limbo. Rupert Brooke's death in the First World War immortalised him at home. It was the same for other war poets like Wilfred Owens or the Canadian, John McCrea, whose poem, *In Flanders Fields*, features on the Canadian $10 bill. Their posthumous reputation was simple; there was no legacy of divided loyalties, no whispered rumours. The Britain to which poets like Siegfried Sassoon and David Jones returned home might, with time, nurse ambivalent feelings towards how 'great' that war was, but such survivors were never viewed as traitors; they could publicly talk about their experiences. Their stories were not blotted out of the national collective memory in their countries or from many histories of the period, with books like T.W. Moody and F.X. Martin's *The Course of Irish History* reducing the Great War to essentially a couple of lines about John Redmond's recruiting speech. It is only in recent years that the war experiences and motivations of Irish men like Ledwidge are being fully explored.

When I try to recall my first encounter with Francis Ledwidge, he is not the only ghost that I need to conjure up. A second ghost lurks in my mind, aged sixteen, the same age that Ledwidge was when he wrote his first proper poem. It is the ghost of my younger self, deeply impressionable and insecure, reaching out blindly towards a future that I could hardly dare imagine. I imagine two very different walks home by sixteen-year-old Irish boys born seventy-two years apart. Both walk the same road north from Dublin City for three miles until they reach my native village of Finglas – then Ledwidge walks on through the darkness of the North Road towards his own village of Slane, on a journey that I can only follow in my imagination. This afterword is not just about Ledwidge's life, his place in Irish literature and the place which he, and the thousands of other Irishmen who died in the First World War, were allotted in history. For me, it is also about how you can encounter a poet in your youth who remains an enduring touchstone in your life.

Ledwidge's walk home as a sixteen-year-old occurs in the autumn of 1902. In Britain, Queen Victoria has consented to finally die, with Edward VII being crowned king in Westminster Abbey. Britain has crushed the Boers in South Africa and Irish passions are rising, fuelled by events like W.B. Yeats's first staging of his propagandist play, *Cathleen Ni Houlihan*. However, I suspect that the new Intoxicating Liquors Act – which reduced the vast array of rural pub licences – was far more widely discussed in the village of Slane in County Meath. Also being discussed there in 1902 was the news of how a local boy, Francis Ledwidge, the likeable son of a widow whose family was much visited by hardship, had landed himself a position as a grocer's apprentice in Rathfarnham, a township on the far edge of the city of Dublin. Grocers have got a raw deal in Irish literature, ever since Yeats depicted them fumbling in greasy tills. Mr W.T. Daly, our dour Rathfarnham grocer, fares little better. A forbidding, unfriendly man (who ran a large business with a grocery shop at one end of his premises and a licensed public house at the other), his gruff manner seems to have merely increased Francis Ledwidge's homesickness.

Sixty years later, another young Irish country person who came to Dublin with dreams of literary fame would also endure the tedium of life behind a shop counter. In *The Country Girls,* Edna O'Brien's 1960s act of rebellion was to secretly dye her bra black in the tiny bedroom above the chemist shop where she worked in Cabra. Ledwidge's act of rebellion in 1902 was less dramatic, but it still permanently closed the door for him on the joys of a retail career.

So consumed with loneliness that he could not sleep in his room above Daly's shop in Rathfarnham, Ledwidge found himself composing his first proper poem, a montage of remembered sights of his native village. After finishing the poem he was filled with restless energy and exhilaration, a new sense of power. Taking his meagre belongings, he crept down through the closed shop, passing its chests of Indian tea, its rows of drawers for spices and grass seeds, its menacing ranks of long boots hanging from the ceiling. He closed the door, terrified that his employer would hear. Walking back down off the foothills of the Dublin Mountains into Dublin City, he found the long straight road, out past Glasnevin cemetery and Finglas village, to Slane. This walk of almost forty miles from Rathfarnham would bring him back to his impoverished mother, his younger brother, Joe, and to the cottage where he had known penury, attempted eviction, starvation and the death of his oldest brother. But within the small rooms of that labourer's cottage there beckoned the irreplaceable sense of home.

In comparison, my own walk at sixteen is decidedly more mundane. In 1975 I walk out the same long road past the tombs of clerical princelings inside the railings of Glasnevin cemetery, and up the steep dual carriageway that replaced the woodland road to Finglas village. My reason for walking home is that I have spent my bus fare and all my savings on the biography of a poet who died in the First World War named Francis Ledwidge. I read this biography by Alice Curtayne with growing curiosity as I walk. At sixteen I need to know that someone else once felt same the way about words as I feel. I crave reassurance, some affinity in my confusion at having become obsessed with the alchemy of verse. I need a hand to reach out – living or dead – and say, '*I have come this way too. Follow your dreams, believe you can write.*'

Ledwidge's rural village of Slane was utterly different from the tough working-class suburb of Finglas. But I realised that Ledwidge would have passed through the main street of Finglas, with the only sounds being his footsteps or a dog barking. A few hundred yards past the police station he would have stopped in the darkness of the North Road to rest on a Royal Mail milestone placed here. Curtayne's biography claimed that during his walk home at sixteen he stopped at every milestone between Dublin and Slane. His fingers would have traced out the distance still to walk, knowing that he was throwing away his mother's hopes of an escape from poverty as he chose to return with nothing except this first poem.

On the night I bought Alice Curtayne's book I went walking and found that – amid all the development that transformed Finglas into a vast, haphazard suburb – that same milestone had miraculously survived. I sat on the stone and closed my eyes to envisage Ledwidge. In my adolescent state, I wanted his ghost to haunt me, his unwritten poems to come through me. I opened my eyes and watched trucks thunder past towards Slane and swore that some night I too would walk out along that road and replicate his journey to Slane. In my adolescent state I convinced myself that, if I retraced his steps and arrived at his cottage at dawn, I would then know how a poet truly felt.

As Curtayne details in her biography (to which I owe a great debt of gratitude for much of the information here), Francis Ledwidge was born to country parents in 1887 in a labourer's cottage in Slane, the second youngest of nine children. His father, Patrick – who died when Ledwidge was four years old – was a migrant agricultural labourer, a profession where you could slave into your eighties and still be referred to as the 'boy'. Ledwidge's cottage was built by the Rural District Council and came with half an acre of garden, presumably to help the inhabitants become self-sufficient. Today his garden in Slane is beautifully kept, as part of a small cottage museum, yet whenever I walk through it I don't think of beauty but of suffering. The orphanages of early twentieth-century Ireland were crammed with children – but not necessarily with orphans. For parents unable to cope, the only option was often to pay a visit to them with your child wrapped in a shawl and walk out with your hands cradling an absence.

Anne Ledwidge's neighbours were clear about her best course of action when her husband died suddenly, leaving her utterly destitute. Francis and his brother Joe, who was only three months old, should be put into an institution while she tried to raise the other children at home. Older prisoners in Stalin's gulags used to talk nostalgically about former incarcerations, then sigh with fond memory and say, 'Ah, but that was a Tsarist jail!' Likewise, Irish orphanages before independence may possibly not have been as bad as the brutalised exploitative factory farms which some Irish religious orders later ran using child slave labour, with little interference from the new state. However, I doubt if any former inmates recalled them nostalgically.

I doubt also if poetry could have survived within Ledwidge had he and his brother been given numbers instead of names behind the bars of an orphanage. However, Anne Ledwidge decided to keep her two youngest sons at home by working during every hour of daylight in the fields around Slane for two shillings and sixpence a day. Francis and Joe – when he grew old enough – would join her after school as she slaved at backbreaking tasks like thinning turnips or potato picking. When darkness fell they could walk back to the cottage, where finally there would be warmth, some food and, if they begged her, stories.

By knitting, washing and mending in winter Anne Ledwidge kept her family together, while managing with great difficulty to educate her eldest son, Patrick, until he secured an office job in Dublin and became the bread-winner. Briefly it seemed that she could spend more time with her young children, but after a spell in Dublin, Patrick returned home, an invalid dying slowly of tuberculosis. Ledwidge wrote about the following four years: 'it was as though God forgot us.' When bailiffs arrived to evict the family they survived only because a doctor testified that Patrick was too ill to be moved. When he died the family lacked the money even for a coffin.

It puzzles me why some people have a mania for making Ledwidge's life picturesque. Certainly the land around Slane is as lush as Flanders is today and a thin cow in Meath would be a tourist. But land is only good if you possess it. There is nothing picturesque for a child in seeing bailiffs come to evict your family or watching your brother die slowly in the back room where you can barely concentrate on his suffering because of your own hunger. To see your mother grow haggard from kneeling in a muddy field, or watch her hands turn blue from scrubbing at other people's washing, or trying to darn by the light of a meagre fire, is not picturesque – no matter how much we prefer to dickey up the rural past as a cosy and simple world.

Large families were instinctive among the poor every-where, not just due to the lack of contraception, but also as a sort of insurance policy because there was a strong probability that not all your children would survive. Child mortality rates were higher in Dublin during Ledwidge's day than they were in Calcutta. My own father remembers, as a boy in 1920s Wexford, being sent out onto the road to wait while his eldest brother slowly died. He rarely speaks of it, but no child could forget such a thing.

What did Ledwidge remember or want to forget about his brother's death? Was he sent out with Joe into the garden so as not to hear the last rasping breath? We don't know because his poems don't actually tell us. He wrote no poems about his brother's coffin, his mother's worn hands, his desperate childhood hunger. Instead we get detailed descriptions of birds, flowers and fauna, all the elaborate paraphernalia that constituted High Georgian verse. We get the middle-class mannerisms of his betters being parroted by this relatively uneducated young man who sat up late at night to write in his cramped cottage, his limbs weary from road repairing or doing the same labouring work as his late father.

Yet, even though Ledwidge never lived long enough to fully rip aside the veil of poetic convention that often separated the artificial language of his poems from the true language of his life, there is something monumentally staggering about the audacity of someone from his class, from his occupation as a farm land and roadworker, even aspiring to being a poet. Edwardian poetry was a gentleman's club, with well-connected ladies occasionally tolerated. Indeed, Ledwidge's own entry into the poetry establishment would be stage-managed by a rich patron, Lord Dunsany. Dunsany, a member of the Meath aristocracy, would generously befriend Ledwidge. He encouraged him, loaned him books and – without any understanding of how outrageous the phrase would seem today – marketed Ledwidge as 'a peasant poet'.

James Joyce, who resolutely embraced the modernity of the twentieth century, was five years older than Ledwidge who, in contrast, seems wrapped up in the dying certainties of the nineteenth century. Often the Joyce family possessed little money either; however, even without cash, they remained middle-class people with connections and breeding. At around the time that Joyce as a precocious student was being praised for his essay on 'Ibsen's New Drama' (with even the great Norwegian playwright himself impressed), Ledwidge was leaving school at thirteen. He left on the morning after he received the Catholic sacrament of confirmation, when childhood ended abruptly. Directly behind his cottage wall he could earn seven shillings a week as a farm boy working from dawn to dusk on the Fitzsimons's farm. However, Anne Ledwidge was ambitious for her children to better themselves and soon a world of grandeur beckoned for Francis.

Today Slane is associated in the public mind with rock music because of an annual concert staged in the natural amphitheatre of the grounds of Slane Castle. Inside this castle U2 waited to play to eighty thousand people. Bruce Springsteen waited to play. Bob Dylan likewise waited his turn and Francis Ledwidge simply waited his chance to wait at table – because that was what trainee houseboys did in Slane Castle while working their way up through a strict servant hierarchy. Slane Castle – heroically restored by its present owner, Lord Henry Mountcharles, after a terrible fire – dominates Slane village. The ordered layout of the village (rare in Ireland) betrays the controlling fist of the Mountcharles family. Some historians claim that the road from Dublin to Slane was straightened by royal order of George IV, who was kicking his heels in Dublin as Prince of Wales, so he might more conveniently reach his mistress, Lady Conyngham, in Slane Castle. It appears that while His Majesty appreciated Irish curves, he didn't much care for Irish bends.

Every summer during its annual rock concert, the young people of Ireland try to do to each other, in quiet corners of the castle grounds, what the future King of England did to Lady Conyngham in more private surroundings indoors. Afterwards when concertgoers traipse back out through the village they pass street benches bearing the words 'Ledwidge Country'. I occasionally wonder if this act by local people to re-colonise the village in the name of a farm labourer is, in some small sense, Slane's way of putting the aristocratic family who ruled the village for centuries in their place. I wonder what the former Marquis of Conyngham (who presumably imagined that Slane was his 'country') would make of local housing estates being named after a penniless boy who – though I doubt if the Marquis was even aware of Ledwidge's brief employment – once worked in his kitchens.

At fourteen Ledwidge had a propensity for mischief and he was soon dispatched back to working in the fields. Not for long, however. His mother soon fixed up an apprentice-ship with a grocer in Drogheda, a town ten miles from Slane. Every Sunday Ledwidge's younger brother Joe accompanied him to a nearby bridge from where Ledwidge walked the rest of the distance to Drogheda. His working hours often lasted until midnight. Drogheda was a small town and his mother wanted to advance his career when the chance came for him to take up his ill-fated, short-lived position with W.J. Daly in Rathfarnham. Looking back now, I suspect that Ledwidge's story of being so stirred by writing his first poem that he abandoned his job and walked home is primarily an attempt to cloak the mundane homesickness of a young country boy who finds himself overwhelmed by the city. However, his mother never sent him back to Dublin or to shopwork. He roamed the fields and lanes seeking work and at last he struck lucky.

A few hundred yards from the famous neolithic burial chamber at Newgrange, several miles from Slane, Ledwidge found employment with a carefree young couple on a farm that today is an open farm where children learn about the countryside. For two years Ledwidge was their 'boy' at £21 a year, helping about the yard, driving their horse and trap and amusing his employers, the Carlyles, by his strange habit of sitting up at their kitchen table late at night to write poems. Paradise rarely lasts, however, and when the Carlyles moved away, Ledwidge found a new career at the age of nineteen.

In 1907 seasonal roadworkers start to be employed in Meath, being paid seventeen shillings and six-pence a week. In starting this new job, Ledwidge was coming up in the world and even acquired a bicycle as he laboured down tiny lanes, with a billycan to brew tea. You can't eat nature, though, and the prospect of more money lured him into starting work as a miner when a copper mine opened in nearby Beaupark. Conditions were dreadful, with ineffective pumps and flooding and accidents being regular occurrences. Ledwidge stood out. Despite his youth, other workers urged him to represent them by presenting their demands for safer conditions. He did so bravely, a union leader organising a strike three years before the Irish socialist leader Jim Larkin famously organised the Dublin workers in their battle against exploitation. The only problem was that when Ledwidge marched in with his demands, his fellow workers melted away, leaving him isolated. He was sacked and marked down locally as a troublemaker.

I wonder what they made of this poet in their midst – his fellow copper miners and road-workers and farm labourers? The notion of a man from his social class even thinking of himself as a writer probably invited ridicule. Growing up in Finglas, I noticed how at talent contest nights in local pubs contestants introduced their songs in Dublin accents but sang them in American ones. It seemed perfectly acceptable to sing about getting your kicks on Route 66, but not about getting kicked on the Finglas dual carriageway. In recent years local rock bands like Aslan have written candidly about Finglas life. Christy Dignam of Aslan even deliberately named one record *Feel No Shame* in reference to the way in which some teachers and parents subtly encouraged job seekers to invent a bogus non-Finglas addresses to enhance their chances. But in the mid 1970s, if someone wanted to write songs it invited ridicule to locate them in Finglas. Likewise, if the young Ledwidge wanted to be taken seriously as a poet, it was unsurprising that there are few poems about such 'unpoetic' themes as the dripping innards of copper mines or the tedium of manual labourer.

When Ledwidge was being sacked from the mines and getting back his job as a roadworker in Meath, another Irish writer who also knocked out a living through manual labour was coughing himself to death in England. Dying of TB, Robert Tressell wondered if the manuscript of his powerful novel *The Ragged Trousered Philanthropists* would ever be read by anyone. The Beaupark copper miners fitted into Tressell's ironic description of un-unionised labour as philanthropists who, for a pittance, would 'toil and sweat at their noble and unselfish task of making money for their employers'.

Tressell's burial place (he was interred in a pauper's grave with twelve others in Liverpool in 1911) remained so obscure that his grave was not located until 1970. In his lifetime none of the three publishers he contacted would even consent to read his sprawling manuscript, which he was unable to get typed. The book was published posthumously in 1914 – the year Ledwidge joined the British Army – and immediately proved a success. But not least among the ironies of a book about exploitation was that this first edition (reprinted for years afterwards) was a deeply distorted and highly censored version of Tressell's manuscript. It was massively cut down, with its revolutionary message sanitised by the middle-class publisher who made the author's twenty-year-old daughter and heir, Kathleen Noonan (Tressell's real surname), sign away the entire rights in perpetuity for a once-off payment of £25. Tressell's daughter never received another penny more in royalties – despite the book eventually selling a million copies and being reprinted over a hundred times as far away as Bulgaria, Japan and Russia. However, half a century later, another publisher condescended to send the elderly Kathleen Noonan a second £25 payment so that she could purchase a television to watch a BBC dramatisation of her father's words.

At the start of the Great War, writers from poor backgrounds were to be tolerated and patronised, but certainly not given their head. After his death, Ledwidge too would find his work censored by his publisher, with a vital anti-militaristic closing line dropped from one posthumously published poem to make it fit into the standard pieties about the war. In his poem about soldiering, 'Soliloquy', published in *Last Songs* in 1918, the published text ends:

> A keen-edged sword, a soldier's heart
> Is greater than a poet's art.
> And greater than a poet's fame
> A little grave that has no name.

This corrupted text still widely circulates on poetry websites. Its circulation even extends to it being carved on a slab at the entrance to the Island of Ireland Peace Park at Messines in Belgium. In inadvertently using this censored text, the Island of Ireland Peace Park omits Ledwidge's last line (only restored years later), which considerably alters the mood of the ending:

> …And greater than a poet's fame
> A little grave that has no name,
> Whence honour turns away in shame.

In death Ledwidge was expected to stay within his box as a simple soldier poet. In 1960s Dublin the poet Eavan Boland found that some people wanting to praise her first book of poems would insinuate glowingly that they were so good you would never know that the author was a woman. Similarly, many readers undoubtedly thought they were praising Ledwidge when stating that his poems were so good you would never know that he was 'a peasant'. Poetry might have opened doors for Ledwidge, but he was expected to play by middle-class notions of what constituted an aesthetic.

I recognise this same unquestioning acceptance of a received aesthetic in my own teenage poems, because at sixteen I never imagined that the lives around me could be subjects for verse. Poetry was meant to be about scenery – like a verbal postcard. At weekends I hitchhiked around the countryside, looking at cows and feeling more poetic for the experience. I was still in my teens when my sister June brought me to a writers' workshop in the People's College in Dublin, an adult education organisation set up by the trade unions. Our tutor, Anthony Cronin, didn't look like a poet – although I discovered that he was one of Ireland's most intelligent voices, whose 'Viewpoint' column in *The Irish Times* was a ray of subversive light in those grey days. Cronin wised me up to the fact that anything within the sphere of human experience was within the realm of poetry. My world of factories and dual carriageways – like Ledwidge's world of copper mines – was suddenly valid, fertile, unexplored poetic territory.

I left school at eighteen and while unemployed for a year tried to establish an arts movement in Finglas, printing broadsheets and holding poetry readings attended by two men and a dog. Then I got a job in a welding rod factory – my debut novel, *Night Shift*, being the welding rod's sole contribution to world literature. Working there, I often thought of Ledwidge, labouring in his copper mine with a sheaf of poems in his pocket. God knows what my kindly fellow factory workers made of their oddball local poet. I stood out, no matter how hard I tried to blend in by cursing harder than anyone there or trying to keep pace in monumental drinking sessions. But could they take me any more seriously than Ledwidge's fellow road-workers could take Ledwidge's notions seriously – even when his poems started to appear – without payment – in the local newspaper, *The Drogheda Independent*? Girls at dances in Meath giggled at the pretensions of this roadworker who adopted 'poetic' dress after his labouring work was over. It would need something special to make locals see him as anything other than a labourer. But that something special was coming – though the ensuing friendship would be viewed with suspicion and misrepresentation for decades to come.

Meath already had a published writer – Lord Dunsany – who lived in a castle in the nearby village that bore his name. Dunsany was famous as a playwright and fiction writer. One day in 1912, when Ledwidge was twenty-four, he posted a hand-written notebook crammed with poems to Dunsany Castle, with a short note wondering if his lordship might find any merit in the enclosed work. Every young poet knows the agony of waiting for validation, for some word from the outside world into which they tentatively send unpublished poems. The process of waking up every morning, hoping – yet half afraid to hope – that the postman will bring news. Months would pass before the poems even reached Lord Dunsany, who had spent the spring in Cannes. But one evening when Ledwidge cycled home from work, a letter awaited him. He opened it and it opened up a whole new world.

On 3 September 1939 – twenty-two years after Ledwidge's death – it is said that the then elderly Lord Dunsany appeared in the kitchens of Dunsany Castle to tell the startled kitchen staff that World War Two had started. Whispers about this momentous event spread through the castle grapevine, with stunned servants barely able to believe what had happened – not the fact that Hitler had invaded Poland, but that his Lordship had actually set foot in his own kitchens.

Without poetry, the lives of Ledwidge and Dunsany would have passed in segregated worlds, twenty miles and yet a million miles apart. But when Dunsany finally received Ledwidge's small copybook of poems and recognised the lyric brilliance of this local roadworker, he sat down to generously write a letter of encouragement. In doing so, he started a friendship that caused suspicion on both sides of a rigid social divide.

Possibly the only good thing to be said about the old English social system was that its subdivisions were blatantly apparent, with P.G. Wodehouse's Bertie Wooster able to neatly divide the English into 'Toffs, Lower Middles and Tough Eggs'. But after winning its independence in 1922, Southern Ireland tried to spin the myth that – as a Republic – we had abolished our class system. Our government ministers did not come from Eton College but from small cabins where guns had been hidden in the thatch. The important university to have graduated from was not Oxford or Cambridge or Trinity College in Dublin, but the Frongoch Internment camp in Wales to which the British had rounded up Republicans after the 1916 Rising. Officially as a state we had turned class on its head – yet, in reality, social class in rural Ireland was intense and all pervasive.

My mother was the daughter of a small Monaghan farmer. Socially this would have put her beyond Ledwidge's reach, because he was landless. But my mother's class needed to know their place too. On one occasion as a girl she visited the daughter of a teacher and her host started to make tea in the china teapot used for visitors. However, the teacher's older daughter stormed into the kitchen to empty the contents of the teapot down the sink, angrily remonstrating that the china teapot should not be produced for the daughter of a mere small farmer. The Irish rural caste system was this pronounced, embedded and multi-layered. If a small farmer's daughter should not be given tea from the good teapot in a teacher's house, then how could a roadworker cycle the twenty miles to Dunsany Castle to meet Lord Dunsany and his wife? With every turn of the pedal on his first trip there, Ledwidge wasn't just crossing a class divide – he was cycling across the fault lines between nationalities.

Although born in London, educated in Eton and Sandhurst and experienced in warfare as a British officer in the Boer War, Lord Dunsany – or to use his prosaic name, Edward John Moreton Drax Plunkett – undoubtedly saw Meath as just as much his home place as Ledwidge did. Dunsany's family in Ireland were able to trace their line back to St Oliver Plunkett, the Catholic Archbishop who was martyred at Tyburn in London in 1681 and whose shrunken head is still inexplicably and grotesquely displayed in Drogheda cathedral. To have one relative hung, drawn and quartered might be enough for most families, but to be born a Plunkett and a Catholic in the seventeenth century was like being born with a silver spoon in your mouth and a silk rope around your neck. Cromwell, who is remembered with no affection in Ireland, hung eleven Plunketts in one day alone. By the eighteenth century Dunsany's branch of the family took the prudent business decision to turn Protestant, which allowed them to retain their estates, while putting another divide between them and what they would term 'the locals'.

By the time that Ledwidge first cycled to meet him, the problem was that no matter how Irish Lord Dunsany saw himself, a groundswell of opinion was starting to regard his entire class as foreigners and would soon refuse to view houses like Dunsany Castle as anything except outposts of foreign occupation. That the same families had lived in them for centuries and felt rooted in the locality counted for nothing. During the War of Independence that followed the First World War, such Anglo-Irish families would suddenly find themselves strangers in a strange country, sometimes given just half an hour to pack a few personal belongings before seeing their houses torched in a campaign of IRA burnings.

Back in the more peaceful era of 1912, when Ledwidge dismounted his bike in the driveway of Dunsany Castle to look up at the great windows of the library where he would soon be given free reign, he must have been acutely aware of such social tensions and suspicions. Were neighbours in Slane laughing behind his back? Would the disbelieving butler at the main door redirect him to the servants' entrance? As he approached the door, what sort of changed future did he imagine? Presumably he dreamed that one day he would move on from such manual tasks as mending roads in Meath, yet surely he never dreamed that the job to replace such work would involved digging rat-infested trenches close to where dying men screamed for a bullet to release them from their agony in No Man's Land. Most certainly he could never have imagined that, within five years, his shattered limbs would be buried in a bomb crater in Flanders and that this fellow-writer, who now held out the hand of friendship, would be deliberately and falsely blamed for his death by Nationalist Ireland.

In St Canice's Boys National School at the age of eleven I first heard of Francis Ledwidge – although his name did not register at the time. But my teacher – a good man who genuinely loved poetry and tried to convey that love to us under seriously difficult circumstances – told us a story about a poet which stayed in my head. He then recited a poem containing an image of a young man isolated by a river. Therefore I think this must have been the Ledwidge poem entitled 'The Excursion' or 'Down by a Lone Long River':

> Down by a lone long river
> They passed me with a frown,
> And I thought of the kind one ever
> Who brings my songs to the town.
>
> And I thought how they will ignore me
> Because of my humble line,
> That I guided the plough before me
> Or bored in the deep wet mine...

Why did these quiet words (one of the Ledwidge's few poems to mention his humble occupations) make such an impression on me? Already my classmates had learnt by heart the mesmeric and Messianic poems of P.H. Pearse – a leader in the 1916 Rising, who, after his execution was promoted to official saint cult status. Pearse's poems, with their macabre death wish and asexual call for self-sacrifice, were the official Nationalist texts. I heard this Ledwidge poem on the sly, on my teacher's own initiative, and it moved me in a way that Pearse's words could not. It felt as if the only person who could really compare himself to Pearse was Christ, and even then Christ would have been found wanting. But to someone like me with a stammer, subjected to sporadic bullying, this image of the poet alone by the river – being snubbed and mocked for having guided the plough and worked in a mine – was fascinating. For years afterwards I could not remember his name, but he was my first outsider. But what really made my classmates sit up in righteous anger was the story about how this young innocent Irish poet was betrayed by an English lord who duped him into wearing a British uniform and therefore getting killed for the wrong cause.

This is how I know that Ledwidge was the poet whose words I heard that day. This story is a total lie – although, as the accepted currency of the day, my genuinely decent teacher believed it. Indeed it is a belief still stubbornly clung to by many. This carefully constructed lie about the relationship between Ledwidge and Dunsany was National-ist Ireland's way of reinforcing the notion of Dunsany as a foreigner and explaining away the retrospective heresy of Ledwidge having died in a British uniform. It ignored the fervent mood of public opinion in 1914 Dublin, when the Irish Rugby Union organised collective recruiting with large numbers of Catholic Nationalists drilling alongside Unionists in Lansdowne Road. It made Ledwidge's death seem like a freak accident, instead of a fate that befell thousands of young Irishmen who enlisted because of a multitude of political beliefs, or because they got caught up in the pressurising collective hysteria or simply because the army seemed the only alternative to chronic poverty – like in the case of numerous Dublin workers still blacklisted by employers after the 1913 Lockout.

Dunsany did not encourage Ledwidge to join the British army, and was annoyed when Ledwidge did so, although at the outbreak of war, Dunsany himself would feel it his immediate duty to enlist. What Dunsany did do, from the summer of 1912 on, was to take the young poet under his wing. He attempted to rid Ledwidge's work of clichés, gave him free use of his library and insisted on providing Ledwidge with an allowance when he was unemployed. He offered to take Ledwidge on his travels to Africa, introduced him to fellow poets in Dublin, sent his poems with strong recommendations to major literary journals and became a father figure to his young neighbour who had lost his own father so young.

Until 1912 Ledwidge had been a local curiosity, published almost weekly in *The Drogheda Independent*. A local girl, Ellie Vaughey, with whom he was in love and who worked in Drogheda, dropped off his submissions at the newspaper office. She was, quite literally, 'the kind one ever' in his poem 'who brings my songs to the town'. Dunsany was to prove a more effective intermediary with editors. Within weeks of their first meeting, *The Saturday Review* in England (edited by a friend of Dunsany) would publish the poem 'Behind the Closed Eye', the first draft of which Ledwidge had written on that night when he ran away as a homesick boy from Daly's grocer's shop in Rathfarnham. Payment was the vast sum of eight guineas – more than seven weeks' wages for Ledwidge as a roadworker at that time.

Poems are one thing, but in Ireland it is cash that makes neighbours sit up. *The Drogheda Independent*, happy to announce the success of their long-standing unpaid contributor, highlighted the detail that would excite most local comment – that the roadworker was being paid at six shillings per line. The future must have looked exhilarating, with Dunsany launching Ledwidge's career by presenting a talk on him to The National Literary Society in Dublin and half his neighbours imagining him to now be a rich man.

But the other half of Slane – the rich half – knew that you couldn't graze cows on the margins of a poem. With Frank and Joe both bringing home a working wage, the bad days were over in the cottage and their mother could stay at home. Compared to a few years before, they were rich. But Ledwidge felt that, in the eyes of Ellie Vaughey's brothers – who farmed half the Hill of Slane and liked the young poet personally – the Ledwidges were still not the class of people that their sister should marry into. However, those first months after Dunsany waved his wand were all the more magical because, just as the world was discovering Ledwidge, he was discovering love. Aged twenty, Ellie radiated gaiety and spontaneity. His poems took on a new vitality, with vivid images of courtship:

> I feel that she will come in blue,
> With yellow on her hair, and two curls strayed
> Out of her combs loose stocks…

But what did she make of him, her faint-hearted lover who may have been more inclined to write things down for a girl rather than actually do things with a girl? Courtship is courtly, but no girl wants to feel that she is made of glass. Ledwidge must have seemed a puzzle to Ellie. On the one hand, he was a step down in class with his labouring job. Yet, on the other hand, he regularly mixed with famous Dublin acquaintances several social classes above her. People like Oliver St John Gogarty – later Buck Mulligan in *Ulysses* – who, taking a caustic view of Dunsany's patronage, branded Ledwidge as Dunsany's pet harper whom he brought around in his wake. For whatever reason, Ellie terminated their relationship and plunged Ledwidge into depression. He told himself that their gulf in class had been too wide, but he would bridge it. By the autumn of 1913 he even landed his first indoor job, as the secretary of the Meath Labour Union in Navan, for which, as a fervent believer in union membership, he had done a great amount of unpaid work.

He learned to type and to use shorthand and dreamed of becoming a journalist, probably with *The Drogheda Independent,* who would surely want such a rising literary star on their paid staff. Liam O'Meara of the Inchicore Ledwidge Society – who has done much work in discovering lost Ledwidge material – unearthed an embarrassingly naïve job application by Ledwidge to the editor of the *Irish Independent,* an overtly poetic appeal destined never to blossom in the hardened cynical newspaper world conjured up by Joyce in *Ulysses.* Any sort of white-collar job would do, provided it gave him the status to win Ellie back. But the Meath Labour Union soon discovered that Ledwidge was better at making up books than at keeping them. Some say he only had the job temporarily and others that he was let go because of poor accounting. But either way, by the spring of 1914 he was back looking for work, supporting himself reluctantly with Dunsany's largesse, and finding that his high-blown literary prose style was not what *The Drogheda Independent* was looking for in a reporter to cover council meetings and country shows. Even worse than that was the fact that every drinker in the Conyngham Arms Hotel in Slane, where Ledwidge liked to drink, knew that Ellie had chosen a new boyfriend – John O'Neill – tall, handsome and full of life, a fiddle-player and singer who – for all of Ledwidge's dwelling on class – possessed little more social status than Ledwidge.

Perhaps land had only been an issue in his head or an excuse on her lips. Drowning his sorrows in the Conyngham Arms, with friends like Matty McGoona and Paddy Healy, if Ledwidge looked into his own heart he may have felt that he had been too caught up in playing at being 'a poet'. Some locals sniggering into their glasses may have felt that, when it came to women, Ledwidge simply didn't have the balls, despite all of his 'six shillings a line' and dressing up in a bow tie and frameless glasses to pretend to be something he was not. Rows took place with fellow drinkers gathered in to listen to the hotel gramophone because of Ledwidge's mood swings. By 1914 Slane was simply too small a goldfish bowl for him to survive in any more.

Not that he stopped throwing himself into local activities. He was even elected as a local public representative on The Navan Rural District Council and Board of Guardians. And elsewhere Dunsany kept pulling strings. To see a first book into print was no easy matter, as James Joyce was discovering at this time. Even though the Dublin publisher Maunsel & Co had finally printed Joyce's *Dubliners* in 1910, they nervously sat on the entire stock for two years before deciding to destroy all copies of the edition at roughly the same time as Dunsany was offering Ledwidge's poems to then in 1912. Maunsel proved equally reluctant to take on Ledwidge and by 1913 Dunsany had found him a better publisher in London. Herbert Jenkins was not only willing to accept Ledwidge's debut volume but – unlike Maunsel – was willing to pay for the privilege. Dunsany travelled to a big African game hunt, then returned home to make the selection for *Songs of the Fields* and write an introduction heralding the appearance of what he termed this 'peasant poet' like a star in the night sky. All they needed now was a publication date.

1913 is often portrayed as a long hot summer when all classes knew their place and the world felt like it would never change. In Ireland, however, it was a year of political turmoil. Three years after Ledwidge had led his short-lived strike in the copper mine, a larger union battle was taking place in Dublin. The Dublin employers, led by William Martin Murphy, locked out the newly unionised workers of the city, led by Jim Larkin, from their places of employment. Dublin families endured the most terrible hardship. Parents tried to ship famished children to Liverpool where English workers might at least feed them, but Catholic priests blocked the gangways, preferring that children die of hunger rather than risk their mortal souls by lodging with Protestants. So many Dublin workers who had been unable to get their job back, would enlist in the British army that three cheers were raised for Jim Larkin in the trenches before the Second Battle of Ypres.

In London, the Irish Party led by John Redmond had finally managed – after twenty-seven years of effort – to see a Home Rule bill for Ireland passed in the British House of Commons. The British House of Lords was still vehemently blocking it, but could not do so forever. Home Rule – an Irish parliament with limited powers for an Irish people – seemed just around the corner, to the consternation of Northern Unionists who swore that they would not recognise this law and openly started to import guns for a new illegal army, the Ulster Volunteers, to oppose it. Not to be outdone – and seeing that the government took no action against the Unionists – in late 1913 the Irish Volunteers was formed by young Nationalists willing to fight, if necessary, behind Redmond for the implementation of Home Rule. Both Francis and Joe Ledwidge threw themselves into organising a Slane corps of the Irish Volunteers. Francis, acting as secretary, was strongly involved in planning a mass rally in the village for 15 August 1914.

We will never know what would have happened had the British government finally dragged Home Rule through the House of Lords, how Carson's Ulster Volunteers would have reacted or what course of action the Irish Volunteers would have taken in the ensuing turmoil. Because, by the time that 15 August dawned, with Ledwidge busying himself to organise the great Slane rally, which was attended by two and a half thousand Volunteers in a field outside the village, the political landscape of Europe had changed forever. The Home Rule bill was about to be shelved until further notice because England had just gone to war with Germany.

When Dunsany rose to speak, as an invited local dignitary, he was dressed differently from how Ledwidge had previously seen him. Not as a fellow poet or a gentleman of leisure, but a soldier. On the first day of war, Dunsany had enlisted in the Royal Inniskilling Fusiliers, being instantly conferred with the rank of captain. Now, as a British army officer, he inspected Ledwidge's line of volunteers and appealed for national unity before the band played both 'God Save Ireland' and 'God Save the King'.

By 1914 land acts had already started to weaken the Anglo-Irish ascendancy class in Ireland. The IRA would soon torch many of their homes, with the Wall Street Crash and the Great Depression meaning that, during the 1930s and 40s, far more Big Houses were simply left to rot, with their roofs stripped for lead and stone from the walls used to mend the roads. The stupor in which some Anglo-Irish families watched this destruction occur wasn't just induced by a lack of money or political power. There was also a lack of will in some cases because the generation of sons meant to inherit these homes had died horrifically in the trenches of Flanders and France.

Lady Fingal, a neighbour of Dunsany, wrote that: 'When the armistice came at last we seemed drained of all feeling. The world we had known had vanished. We hunted again but ghosts rode with us. We sat at table and there were absent faces.' The call to serve in the British army was inbred within this class. After all, they had the most to lose. Therefore there was no surprise at Dunsany's decision to join up. But how the Irish Volunteers would react to war in Europe was far less clear-cut. For one thing, the Volunteers were not a united force but a rainbow coalition of Nationalist opinions. Despite the paramilitary trappings and drilling, most members were staunchly constitutional Redmondite Nationalists. However, the IRB (forerunner to the IRA), who were in some key positions, wanted full independence and would happily use German aid to get it.

Ledwidge at first possessed a romantic notion that the British government would ask the Irish Volunteers to defend the Irish coast against invasion, with Irish Volunteers and Ulster Volunteers uniting in this common cause. Soon John Redmond had a different idea, however, feeling that the war was a chance for the Irish nation to show themselves worthy of being granted self-government by fighting for Belgium, as one small Catholic nation helping another. Two months after the war started he made a speech that split the Volunteer movement asunder. In it he declared that the duty of young Volunteers was to enlist in the British army to help defend the freedom of Ireland that would be guaranteed under Home Rule once the nuisance of this short war was over.

Redmond wasn't alone in his recruiting call. A huge propaganda machine swung into action, with the Catholic Church throwing its full weight into drumming up recruits. Word came from every pulpit that it was a Catholic duty to defend Belgium, where nuns were being raped. If the first casualty of war is truth, then nuns are always in the first line of casualties. The same spurious rumour of the rape of nuns was heard from pulpits again in 1936 when the Spanish Civil War started. Indeed, it was a propaganda tool dating back to the Middle Ages, when it was used to justify the slaughter of Jews. IRB men within the Volunteers, like P.H. Pearse, denounced Redmond's call, but their dissent only swayed a small fraction of the membership. Thirteen and a half thousand such dissidents broke away to form a splinter group who retained the name of the Irish Volunteers. The overwhelming majority of one hundred and seventy-five thousand men opted to side with Redmond, renaming themselves as the National Volunteers. Almost to a man, the Meath Volunteers backed Redmond's recruiting call. Once again Ledwidge stood resolutely against popular opinion. With his brother, Joe, and just four others he walked out of the local hall when the Slane corps threw their support behind Redmond.

Ledwidge seemed absolutely clear in his mind that Redmond was wrong to call for recruits. But he was fighting a losing battle with public opinion and was an utterly lone voice when he attended the next meeting of the Navan Rural District Council and Board of Guardians. At this meeting a notion was debated, condemning those Volunteers who had broken away from Redmond as being dangerous, unrepresentative militants. Ledwidge, who spoke against the motion, was jeered and shouted down, being called pro-German and a coward. Outrage ensued when he correctly commented that while the men sitting around him had previously passed resolutions which supported Redmond's call, 'when the motor cars came next day for them to join the army, I did not see them go'.

You can bet your life that he didn't see them enlist. Unlike Dunsany's class, who were trying to perpetually retain a foot in two countries, the prosperous Catholic burghers of towns like Navan possessed little inbuilt sense of duty to anything except their businesses. As a class they might have little intention of going near any war, but they would not be lectured by a whippersnapper unemployed roadworker with hardly an arse in his trousers. If Ledwidge was any sort of true Irishman, instead of a pro-German coward, then they maintained that he could show his love for Ireland by enlisting.

Five days after being the sole dissenting voice at the Navan Board of Guardians; within weeks of resigning from the

Slane Volunteers in protest at the notion of recruitment; haunted by constant sighting of Ellie Vaughey being escorted around Slane by her new beau, John O'Neill, while locals sniggered at Ledwidge's failure to win her; without even a steady job to show for all his recent success as a poet; with streaks of depression and fierce pride in turmoil within him, Ledwidge did what many of the loud local voices who supported Redmond shied away from doing. He decided that Europe's war was Ireland's war and therefore his war too. He came to Dublin unbeknownst to Dunsany, entered the gates of Richmond Barracks and enlisted in the same regiment as Dunsany – the Royal Inniskilling Fusiliers. It was the most Irish regiment in the army, although it was not fully Irish, because Britain would never risk that.

When he walked back out of these gates as a soldier he had not been miraculously elevated to the rank of captain like Dunsany. Ledwidge was a private, starting from square one like always, on wages of seven shillings a week – a shilling more than the rate of pay for a single line of poetry in London. After six months of military service he would have earned what *The Saturday Review* paid for the first poem of his that they published. Later, when asked why he enlisted, he replied, 'I joined the British army because she stood between Ireland and an enemy common to our civilisation and I could not have her say that she defended us while we did nothing at home but pass resolutions.'

When news of his action reached the Navan Guardians, they were deeply impressed and recanted their accusation that Ledwidge was pro-German. They declared him in fact 'a real patriot, the Guardian Angel of Ireland's future'. Everybody knew that the war would only be a short matter of months, but I wonder if at least a few of the Navan Guardians secretly wished that it might even stretch to the improbable length of one year, so as to spare them Ledwidge's speeches about the rights of labour.

Even today, Ledwidge's reasons for joining the British army rankle with many Irish people. It is torturously debated or whispered about in some quarters in the same shocked disapproving tones as if we had discovered that our favourite maiden great aunt had contracted syphilis during her flower arranging classes. For decades this awkward fact dogged how Irish people related to Ledwidge. To accept that he enlisted – along with many of the more than two hundred thousand other Irishmen whose motives were written out of the re-scripted narrative of Irish history after independence – not out of any love of England but from a sense of duty to Ireland, was a heresy against the consensus opinion which downplayed and distrusted Irish involvement in the Great War.

Successive Irish governments were never able to knock down the Irish National War Memorial Gardens at Island-bridge, near Richard Barracks in Dublin – designed by Sir Edwin Lutyens in memory of the almost fifty thousand Irish soldiers killed during that war. But for years (until being beautifully restored around two decades ago) those eight-hectare gardens were allowed to become so overgrown that anyone stumbling upon them by the Liffey might imagine they must have belonged to some lost civilisation. The roll books of the dead kept there contain the names of other men even more fervently committed to Irish Nationalism than Ledwidge was. Some survived to express these Republican beliefs in different ways. Tom Barry – later one of the IRA's most effective and ruthless flying column leaders – enlisted in the British army in 1915 and was fighting in Meso-potamia (part of present day Iraq) when he got news of the Easter Rising.

Emmet Dalton, who became one of Michael Collins's right hand men in the IRA during the War of Independence, had likewise been in the British army in the First World War. It was Dalton who cradled the dying Collins in 1922 when

Collins was ambushed and shot by IRA irregulars opposed to the treaty he made with England, which had the support of a majority of Irish people. A rumour was later spread that Dalton himself had shot Collins because – seeing as he had once served in the British army – he was a useful scapegoat who would always be regarded by some as a traitor. Likewise, the easiest solution to explain away the fact that Ledwidge enlisted was to invent the rumour that blamed Dunsany. As late as 1960 the Abbey Theatre even staged a play that distorted their relationship and added currency to the lie that my honourable schoolteacher believed.

In fact, the last thing that Dunsany needed in Richmond Barracks was for Ledwidge to turn up. Dunsany was furious, refusing to speak to him at first. For a start, while Dublin literary circles might allow a space where this unusual friendship across the class divide could be indulged, friendship between commissioned officers and common soldiers had no place in the regimented structure of barracks life. It can hardly have met with universal approval in the officers' mess that this new captain was becoming overly familiar with a mere private. Not that Ledwidge could ever be accused of being overly familiar. Throughout their friendship he referred to Dunsany as 'Your Lordship' in letters. Ledwidge remained eternally respectful and grateful to Dunsany on a personal basis, while at the same time in *The Drogheda Independent* he railed against Slane being filled with 'West Britons who ape the aristocracy like the frog in the fable'.

The popular perception of their relationship is of one between a young man and a far older one, but less than a decade divided their ages. If Dunsany was annoyed at Ledwidge's enlisting in the army, he continued to play his role as patron with the same generosity. He tried to find Ledwidge a room in Dublin to write in and invited comment by advising him on poems in his officer's quarters. Gogarty's snide reference to Ledwidge as Dunsany's pet harper must have been mild compared to other comments in the officers' mess. Alice Curtayne's labour of love biography of Ledwidge contains fifty references to Lord or Lady Dunsany. But while Dunsany's own writings contain numerous references to Ledwidge, the sole biography of Dunsany contains a mere two references to Ledwidge, one of which suggests that Dunsany must have been rather embarrassed by this troublesome army private.

Dunsany outlived Ledwidge by four decades, dying in 1957. Ledwidge was not the only writer that he influenced, with Jorge Luis Borges working the title of Dunsany's story, *Idle Days on the Yann*, as the twenty-seventh title in his *The Library of Bable*. Arthur C. Clarke regularly corresponded with him in the 1940s and 1950s and other science fiction and fantasy writers like Michael Moorcock, David Eddings and Peter S. Beagle cite him as a major influence. In a writing career of over fifty years he wrote scores of books and plays that reached an audience that his protégé could never have dreamed of. Yet the irony is that, when he is remembered at all today in Ireland, it is generally as an appendix to the tragic Ledwidge narrative. In a curious way both Ledwidge and Dunsany were victims of class prejudice, because Dunsany had encountered a reverse snobbery when he started to write. In the public mind writers were meant to starve between publishers' advances, not wander off to play chess internationally whenever the mood took them. If some people doubted if true literature could spring from a labourer's cottage, then others within Ireland felt that it could not spring from a castle either, that an author with such wealth had to be a mere dilettante.

If one had to strike a discordant note about the relationship between Dunsany and Ledwidge it would be to say that while Dunsany was an immensely imaginative prose writer, he was a mediocre poet. Yeats advised poets to keep company with their betters. In relying so heavily on Dunsany's opinions, Ledwidge never had time to learn what Joyce instinctively knew, that creativity has little place for sentiment or patronage, the survival of the intellectually fittest eventually requires you to bite any hand that feeds you. Incidentally, one of the few connections between Joyce and Ledwidge is that they shared a human failing of many young poets – both borrowed money from the ever generous Irish writer AE (George Russell) and neither paid it back – although Ledwidge had Dunsany to insist on paying it back on his behalf.

Whatever his motives, Ledwidge was now a soldier. So how was his war? It was protracted, bloody and disillusioning without ever quite breaking his spirit. He wrote in impossible conditions, with short poems scribbled on any piece of paper available, often lost or illegible after being soaked in mud in his uniform before he could post them to a safer place. He saw no shortage of action. He was injured and court-martialled, he shot a Turkish sniper and crouched at night in trenches while the sky blazed with flares and a bullet awaited any movement. Yet what is remarkable is how little of this horror permeated into his poems. He saw the barbed wire of No Man's Land and remembered the fences of fields at home. He saw a lone bird on a blackened tree stump and imagined that he heard whole flocks warbling by the Boyne. Partly this may have been because the Georgian lexicon of pastoral innocence was simply unequipped to describe the horror of the Somme – summed up by Paul Fussell, in his study of the war poets, as 'one of the most interesting (moments) in the whole long history of human disillusion'. Ledwidge never lived long enough to acquire the stripped down anti-poetic language of someone like T.E.

Hulme (who also died in Flanders), who summed up the futile limbo of the trenches in his one war poem:

> Behind the line, cannon, lying back miles.
> Before the line, chaos.
> My mind is a corridor. The minds around me are
>   corridors.
> Nothing suggests itself. There is nothing to do but
>   keep on.

In Richmond Barracks in Dublin, Dunsany pulled strings to allow Ledwidge to avoid the slog of basic training. Within weeks he had earned himself a lance corporal's stripe, allowing him more freedom to visit friends and other writers in Dublin. But he suffered the first wound of war when reading a local Meath newspaper sent to him at Richmond Barracks. Among the small announcements, details were given of Ellie's wedding to his rival, John O'Neill. The marriage seemed hastily arranged, with the newlyweds inviting comment by planning to immediately move away to Manchester.

As Ledwidge threw himself into training that soon became more rigorous, I wonder whose face he saw as he plunged his bayonet into the practice sack while drill masters screamed instructions on how to twist the blade in your enemy's guts. Was it John O'Neill's face or his own, the cowardly lover who had been too wrapped up in his poetry and flights of fancy? A good stanza might flatter girls, but a hurried marriage might suggest that they preferred to be seen more as flesh and blood. Ellie was gone. He tried to get involved with another local girl in Meath, Lizzy Healy, but she soon grew tired of a long-distance courtship by post that fell considerably short of the X-rated correspondence course that Joyce and Nora Barnacle had established for separated lovers.

Ledwidge was about to follow the woman he had loved to England. Dublin crowds gathered to give their boys a send-off, with bands playing and girls stealing kisses. All Ireland seemed behind them. Ledwidge wrote: 'They cheered, they swarmed after us, they broke our ranks – they jostled us, linked arms with us, thrust apples, cigarettes, lucky trinkets, rosaries, scapulars, packets of sweets into our hands.'

In Basingstoke in England Ledwidge's regiment endured more intense training. He was making an impression, spreading his wings away from the claustrophobia of Slane. One fellow soldier, Bob Christie from Belfast, who became a great army friend, noted his intelligence, how 'he had but to appear on a barrack square for the whole place to come alive'. Ledwidge and Christie became inseparable, hatching plans to write plays together. Their friendship summed up the contradictions of the war, with Christie being a staunch Unionist whose political opinions were the exact opposite of Ledwidge's. The Unionist leader Carson was as enthusiastic about herding his followers into the slaughter of war as the Nationalist leader Redmond was. Christie, however, had joined up more from a sense of adventure, postponing plans to emigrate to Canada. Both men steadfastly refused to allow political differences to interfere with their friendship. Dunsany was also stationed in Basingstoke but enjoyed the luxury of a large house where he could stay with his wife, with Ledwidge given a room to write in when off duty. Here both men worked together to correct the page proofs of *Songs of the Fields*. Herbert Jenkins had finally decided to launch his new poet. Publishers love angles and with Ledwidge in the army, Jenkins felt that he could grab media attention by crudely emphasising his impoverished background in publicity.

Now it was time for war wound number two. Just before Ledwidge's regiment was due to leave for the Dardanalles, he had a deeply terrifying dream and soon afterwards heard that an unhappy Ellie had died in childbirth, seven months into a failed marriage. The war wasn't getting any better and – for him – it hadn't yet begun. Gloom swamped him, throwing him into acute depression. If he had not lost her then, he might never have joined the army and she might be alive still. Now, haunted by such thoughts, he started to lose the companionship of the two fellow soldiers he most cared for. The first was Dunsany, who had watched out for Ledwidge during the past year. But with the regiment being shipped off into the wholesale slaughter of Gallipoli, the army was not keen to needlessly lose an officer of Dunsany's experience. To his own fury, and the disappointment of his men, who found him different from the general run of officers, Dunsany was ordered to report to the safety of Derry to train new recruits. Ledwidge would sail into battle without him.

Then, amid the chaos of the catastrophic landings at Gallipoli, Ledwidge lost the companionship of his new friend, Bob Christie. It is hard to imagine a more disastrously inept military campaign than the murderous nine-month-long fiasco that occurred at Gallipoli and led to the deaths of almost three thousand Irish soldiers. In 1915 these Irishmen formed part of a massive flotilla who started being dumped at dawn onto a succession of beaches in the Dardanelles. Huge numbers never reached the sands, mown down in clusters by machine-gun fire as they rushed forth or were pushed out onto on the gangplank to fall into the shallow waves that turned completely red around them. Some were landed in the wrong places with absolutely no shelter. Others landed on initially poorly defended beaches with nearby abandoned villages at their mercy but were denied an easy victory by being ordered not to advance until they had linked up with their comrades being mown down like flies elsewhere. The Cambridge poet Rupert Brooke felt the approaching assault on Gallipoli would be the happiest day of his life, but expired from a mosquito bite two days before it happened.

Ledwidge and Christie spent an entire day onboard ship, watching successive waves of troops being landed and charging up the beach as sitting ducks for the Turks, who controlled the rising ground beyond the sands. It was pitch dark before Ledwidge made it ashore. By then the invasion plan was already in tatters. It proved impossible to even dig proper trenches in the sandy soil, but Ledwidge's D company made a shallow hole to crouch in and shelter from the gunfire. Curtayne describes how any water that reached them was rust stained and smelled of petrol. Dysentery broke out, flies swarmed mercilessly around scorched faces. After being held in reserve for a week they were pitched into battle, a mad, unsuccessful scramble towards the Turkish guns, followed by a tattered retreat. Ledwidge called it hell, writing that 'no man thought he would ever return'. Of the two hundred and fifty men in D company, only seventy-six returned. Carrying scores of wounded back while under fire, he discovered Christie among them. They exchanged a quick word before Ledwidge waded back into the slaughter and Christie was taken away on a ship, his soldiering days done.

Although the Irish formed only a small component of the slaughter at Gallipoli, the number of Irish killed or crippled reached into every village and every social class, leaving huge emotional wounds that could often not be spoken of in the newly independent state. Hugo Hamilton summed up this collective national amnesia with the title of his memoir, *The Sailor in the Wardrobe*. It refers to the photograph of his grandfather in British military uniform which Hamilton's father (a fanatical Irish speaker and Nationalist) kept in a locked wardrobe in his Dublin house in the 1960s, unable to throw out the photograph while desperate to pretend that it didn't exist.

The fiasco of Gallipoli lasted two months for Ledwidge, with constant bombardments and attacks by Turkish snipers, one of whom he shot dead while on watch duty. Finally they retreated by boat to the Greek island of Lemnos. After two weeks of rest there they were tossed into war again. This time they marched through Serbia, where a scorched earth policy meant they were soon on starvation rations and experiencing frostbite in the depth of winter. The scenery was beautiful, but, as Ledwidge knew from birth, you cannot eat scenery.

Here, while existing on a quarter tin of bully beef per day, a parcel finally reached him. It was *Songs of the Fields* – his first book, and the only one that he would ever hold in his hands. The second poem in the book was 'Behind the Closed Eye'. How far away Slane had seemed at sixteen on the night when he wrote the first draft of that poem above Mr Daly's shop in Rathfarnham. As a boy that night in Rathfarnham, Ledwidge surely thought that he understood homesickness, but back then he had been able to make his long walk home to Slane. However, there was no road home from Serbia. To turn your back on the army as a soldier was to be shot, and the British army was remarkably fond of shooting Irish soldiers for desertion, be they shell-shocked, disorientated or simply detailed from their unit amid the fighting.

I suspect that, amid his pride at holding a published book, he felt the frustration that all new writers feel, because by the time your debut finally appears you have generally rejected this earlier work and moved on. Its weaknesses were apparent to him. He feared the worst from the critics, but in fact many London papers went crazy for this 'stream of pure crystal' written by a poet-soldier. Dunsany's introduction described him as a peasant and Jenkins's blurb referred to him – to both Ledwidge's and Dunsany's horror – as having worked as a road 'scavenger'. However, the packaging worked, with the first edition sold out within weeks, a second printing planned and the publisher keen for a second volume.

Ledwidge wasn't worried about negotiating an advance; he simply wanted to receive a supply of writing paper as he froze with his comrades in the Serbian hills. He was too short of writing materials to even send copies of new poems to Dunsany. Snow storms came and then freezing rain. They cut their losses and retreated ninety miles in teaming rain, with the Bulgarian army hounding them with bayonet charges. Alice Curtayne relates how he passed a Serbian girl shivering with cold after being separated from her family in the chaos. He gave her his great coat, forgetting that his reading glasses were in the pocket.

Their unit had been given up for dead long before they reached Salonika, where the other solders could not believe that any of them were alive. Ledwidge collapsed, mentally and physically exhausted, his back so crippled with rheumatic arthritis that he could no longer stand up. A succession of hospitals followed, mainly in Egypt, before he boarded a ship that briefly docked in Naples. The Meath roadworker was seeing more of the world than he could have ever imagined as a boy. Finally, in a cruel irony, he was transferred to a hospital in Manchester – the same city where Ellie had died in the agony of childbirth. He had seen so much horror, yet this was the tragedy that his mind dwelled on. Elegies for Ellie poured out, with him claiming in a letter: '*I have no rest because of Ellie, even yet*'. However, at least he felt sure that his fighting days were over. He was badly injured and sick of the war. Bob Christie, who was now discharged, told him how to fake the extra injuries that would ensure his escape. But Ledwidge seemed to genuinely believe that no doctor who heard the story about all he had endured would send him back. This shows that, despite his travels, he was still an innocent. An empire at war could not risk a valuable asset like Dunsany, but empires have an infinite appetite for the fodder of unimportant foot soldiers.

However, safe in hospital and with rave reviews coming in, life must have seemed reasonably bright as Easter Monday dawned in 1916. But a few hours later a small faction of the marginal rump Irish Volunteers – who had become a familiar and mocked sight as they regularly paraded through Dublin – stopped halfway down the main street and stormed into the General Post Office. An Irish flag was raised and the poet P.H. Pearse read the proclamation of a Republic to bemused onlookers. To the bafflement and anger of the city's populace, an insurrection had begun. Vastly outnumbered, and with the German military support they had been promised not materialising, the leaders knew that they hadn't a chance. But they were putting down a marker, changing the agenda with their blood and the blood of a lot of civilian onlookers. Suddenly Ireland was playing by a new set of rules.

The final Soviet Cosmonauts sent into space showed great courage in spending longer away from earth in their epic orbit than almost anyone else before them. They had reason to believe that upon their return they would be acclaimed as heroes of the Union of Soviet Socialist Republics. The problem was that by the time they finally returned to earth they found that the Soviet Union had vanished, its political borders having disintegrated in their absence. The home they came back to might have physically looked the same, but unbeknownst to them they had become citizens of a different country. As a battle-scarred war veteran lying in hospital in Manchester and reading reports of the short-lived uprising, Ledwidge must have felt something similar. The dissident rump of Volunteers who had broken away from Redmond (supported by almost nobody in Meath except Ledwidge and his brother), the lunatic fringe of toy soldiers ridiculed for parading around Dublin when real men were fighting elsewhere, had suddenly risen. Or at least a section of that rump had. Splits and confusions, with mobilisation orders issued and then counter orders issued, meant that less than a thousand men were taking over Dublin buildings, using amateurish military tactics.

Although militarily naïve, Pearse and the others understood that if the actual fighting could not be won without the promised help of the German army (the 'gallant allies in Europe' referred to in the proclamation), the propaganda war might be just as important. They didn't feel any need for a popular mandate – indeed, the citizens of the Dublin slums generally ignored their insurrection, being too busy getting on with the more important business of looting every shop in sight. A popular mandate might only come if the British military was stupid enough to over-react in their retribution. And having endured Gallipoli, Ledwidge knew that the British military could teach a masters degree course in unsubtle stupidity.

There is an extreme irony in the fact that Ledwidge, who longed to fight for Ireland, should be wounded in Serbia, while Dunsany, who longed to fight against the Germans, was wounded in the 1916 Rising in Dublin. Dunsany was home in Meath on leave from Derry that Easter. Indeed, Ledwidge had planned to come home from Manchester too but was now unable to travel as all boats were cancelled because of the Rising. On hearing about the Rising, Dunsany had travelled to Dublin to help quell it. It was there that he received his only war wound, shot in the face when insurgents tried to commandeer his car. Dunsany lay in a Dublin hospital while the city blazed around him. It says much for their friendship that when Ledwidge began writing laments for the executed leaders of the Rising – who included fellow poets he regarded as friends – Dunsany could recognise their merit despite being left with a permanent scar which partly paralysed his face. The British proved less forgiving than Dunsany. With much of Dublin reduced to rubble, they commenced immediate court martials and executions. Some death sentences seemed obvious, like P.H. Pearse, who had declared himself president of the provisional government. Others seemed merely spiteful, like the young and unimportant Willie Pearse, who had done little except to try and be the same sort of faithful younger brother that Joe Ledwidge tried to be to Francis. Each execution proved a hammer blow against British rule, with public sympathy swinging behind the insurgents. The widespread arrest of political activists, many with no connection to the Rising, helped to radicalise public opinion. Later, the same Dublin crowds who once cheered Ledwidge as he marched off to war, and who had jeered and pelted the insurgents as they surrendered, would greet each survivor of the Rising as a hero when they returned from the Frongoch Internment camps in Wales, which had been emptied of German prisoners of war to accommodate the Irish internees. By that time Ledwidge would be in the midst of the final military campaign that led to his death.

When Ledwidge eventually managed to reach Dublin from Manchester in the immediate aftermath of the Rising, most of the leaders had already been executed. However, further trials were taking place in the barracks to which he was ordered to report. The sight that greeted him in the main square was of fellow Irishmen caged behind barbed wire, awaiting shipment to Frongoch. Atrocities had been committed within those barracks walls, and two days after Ledwidge arrived, the last of the executions occurred, when the wounded socialist labour union leader, James Connolly, whom Ledwidge admired, needed to be strapped upright in a chair in nearby Kilmainham Jail so that British soldiers could shoot him.

Ledwidge must have felt an acute sense of isolation. The men held in cages in the barracks, with whom he felt common cause and some of whom he knew from his Irish Volunteers days, now regarded him as an enemy. In the barracks itself he rowed with the commanding officer, arguing that when he fought on two fronts abroad he had been fighting for Ireland, just like them. The furious officer threatened to report his insubordination, refused his request for additional leave and told him to report to the barracks in Derry in several days' time.

Ledwidge was on course for a court martial when he stopped in Slane to spend a precious few days with his family. His appearance there caused a sensation but at heart he was morose, sick of the war and finding, as he said privately, that death was now as interesting to him as life. In the cottage garden, he told his brother Joe, 'If I heard the Germans were coming in over our garden wall, I wouldn't go out to stop them now.' God knows the number of men he had seen buried, but his heart was in the grave of Ellie Vaughey, whose body had been brought back to Slane. How many surreptitious walks did he take up to the graveyard on the Hill of Slane to look around him and think of how his world had changed in the short time since he and Ellie used to meet for trysts by the river? However, it wasn't just Ellie that he was writing laments for now. His family could not get him to discuss the war. What he wanted them to do was listen to his latest poem.

When the American monk and poet Thomas Merton was once asked for his star sign, he replied that all men are born under the same sign, the sign of contradiction. Here was a lance corporal in the British army, barely two weeks after the Easter Rising, publicly reciting a lament for a fellow poet, Thomas McDonagh, who had been executed by soldiers in the same uniform as Ledwidge himself.

He shall not hear the bittern cry
In the wild sky, where he is lain,
Nor voices of the sweeter birds
Above the wailing of the rain.

Nor shall he know when loud March blows
Thro' slanting snows her fanfare shrill,
Blowing to flame the golden cup
Of many an upset daffodil.

But when the dark cow leaves the moor,
And pastures poor with greedy weeds,
Perhaps he'd hear her low at morn
Lifting her horn in pleasant meads.

This single poem allowed Ledwidge to occupy a curious place in the official poetic hierarchy of my school days. McDonagh was probably the best of the three poets who were among the seven signatories of the proclamation of the republic, but McDonagh's poetry is largely forgotten. It is through this poem, written by an Irishman in a British uniform, that McDonagh lives on in the public imagination. The poem also managed to link Ledwidge tangentially to the Easter Rising. Without it, he would have been banished from public sight like the two hundred thousand Irishmen who fought with him.

The fact that the Easter Rising was one of the few armed revolts ever to be led, in part at least, by middle-class poets may explain both its general incompetence as a military operation and also its immediate mythologising. Two of the poets, Patrick Pearse and Joseph Mary Plunkett, were so far removed from reality that survivors of the Rising, like Desmond Fitzgerald and Earnest Blythe, report them having a conversation during the Rising about how, if they achieved victory alongside the Germans, the Irish people would happily accept a German Catholic prince as their new king, most especially because such a German would favour ruling in the Irish language. History and literature became intermingled in the cult of idolatry created around the three poets of the Rising. Pearse was no street fighter, but had the literary sense to get his retaliation in first. The British might shoot him, but he had already planted a number of powerful poems like depth charges primed to go off and rally support behind shrewder leaders like Michael Collins, who would return from that Welsh internment camp with a better understanding of how to fight dirty.

Joseph Mary Plunkett left behind one memorable poem – a piece of high Catholic mysticism, 'I See His Blood Upon the Rose', that allowed him immediate elevation into being not just a Nationalist icon, but also a Catholic one. Thomas McDonagh had the most vitality and humour of the three of them. If Pearse appears to come across in some of his poems as a repressed gay, McDonagh was an intelligent figure of unrepressed gaiety. Co-opted onto the military council only at the last minute, none of his own poems seemed sufficiently pious to politically brainwash Irish children in schoolbooks. This was where Ledwidge proved useful. Being killed in the wrong uniform should have sealed the official perception of Ledwidge. Here was a poet whose Nationalist credentials would always be questioned, a poet who would have officially vanished from the official canon had he not produced this popular elegy with which, by proxy, they could represent McDonagh.

Ledwidge's Nationalist sentiments in the poem were sufficiently non-ambiguous to be drilled into generations of schoolchildren. It would never be enough to elevate him among the saints like Pearse and Plunkett, but it prevented him from being consigned to hell. The poem allowed him a brief cameo appearance as a penitent kneeling to touch the cloak of one of the pantheon of Republican icons whose eyes stared out from every school corridor. Ireland allowed him to express his repentance, as a venial but not a mortal sinner, from the margins of our schoolbooks, as an awkward historical anomaly, quarantined in limbo.

Increasingly he was in limbo during that last year of his life. When he finally reached Derry from Slane, after a stop-over with Bob Christie in the heart of Unionist Belfast, he was court-marshalled for being late and for his insubordination in Dublin. He lost his stripe but didn't care. The innocent Bambi-like country boy dreaming in the fields of Meath was gone. Here was a disillusioned man, drinking wildly when he got money and standing drinks for every soldier around him. The ever-concerned and helpful Dunsany returned to Derry, nursing his injuries from the Rising, and helped Ledwidge prepare a second book, *Songs of Peace*, with poems first scribbled in Serbia and elsewhere being re-worked in the small sanctuary of a room that Dunsany provided.

In mid-December his name was posted up among those soldiers ordered to join the fighting in France. He was allowed to make one final brief visit home to Slane. Alice Curtayne describes how his ever-faithful brother Joe mistimed a message on the final evening and arrived home to spy Francis already in a car being driven away. Francis wrote to Joe that his troop train might stop at Drogheda on the next day for a few moments and they could properly say good-bye. His brother waited for two days but the train never came.

The 'great push' across France and into Flanders was Ledwidge's third and final battlefront and as terrible as the previous two. If Gallipoli's heat had been appalling, here in the trenches he knew months of intense cold, where drinking water had turned to ice by the time it reached them. But he wrote more than ever, not just poems but letters to new admirers of his work. How strange those two conflicting lives must have seemed. To be a minor celebrity with American professors writing to you, yet at the same time to know that you were a cheap hunk of meat to be held back or sacrificed at whatever time his superiors decided.

He wrote in one letter: 'I may be dead before this reaches you, but I will have done my part. Death is as interesting to me as life. I have seen so much of it. I am always homesick. I hear the roads calling, and the hills, and the rivers wondering where I am.' He lived in a landscape as close to hell as any of us can imagine. Today the town of Ieper – where the remarkable In Flanders Fields Museum is located – is utterly beautiful, but it is also a complete architectural forgery, with its ancient streetscape restored brick by brick after being utterly flattened in 1917. By the time Ledwidge reached there, the only thing left standing was one side of the clock tower.

After all the propaganda about poor Catholic Belgium, Ledwidge would finally get to see the place, advancing on the Germans who were destroying everything in their retreat across France, poisoning wells and trying to ensure that – where possible – not a brick was left standing. The landscape of Flanders is flat anyway, but when Ledwidge finally got there it must have seemed like it stretched into eternity. Before crossing the border from France, Ledwidge and his comrades huddled underground in cellars in the devastated city of Arras, enduring intense artillery bombardments. The war might have turned against the Germans, but here the

Germans were giving it every shot they had. Finally the order to advance came, with four miles of trenches being seized from the Germans, who countered repeatedly in the weeks that followed. This time the wounded in No Man's Land didn't call out for days for a bullet to end their misery. The mud was so deep they simply sank into it and drowned.

Ledwidge was spared and they pushed on into better country. Summer came suddenly and nature broke out somehow behind the lines. He wrote: 'This is my birthday. I am spending it in a little red town in an orchard. Although I have a conventional residence I sleep out in the orchard and every morning a cuckoo comes.' Writing this letter in the sunshine, it must have seemed possible that perhaps he would survive after all. Against all the odds he imagined that he had lived to see thirty and now his company was being held in reserve away from the fighting. However, it wasn't his birthday when he wrote the letter. In Ledwidge's time birthdays were for rich people who could afford to celebrate them. He had its date wrong in his mind by two months. By the time his real birthday came, he would be dead.

At the start of July his company crossed into Belgium. He was due leave but the army had no intention of granting it. The third battle of Ypres (Ieper) was being planned, the bombardment commencing, the standard foreplay before the slaughter of soldiers charging enemy lines. But Ledwidge's luck seemed in on the morning of 31 July in horrific weather, when the terrible push began with thirty thousand men in British uniforms either killed or wounded on that first day for the gain of just one hundred yards. The dead on both sides in that day alone amounted to over eleven thousand. His unit were held back behind the lines, labouring in sodden mud all afternoon as they tried to lay down a wooden track as a road for the wounded to escape. Tea had just been issued in the rain, with Ledwidge and his companions pausing to drink the scalding beverage, when a stray shell landed, killing him and the others outright.

They were buried hastily in the crater made by the shell and it was not until 1919 – when an eerie calm had settled around the now featureless and rat-infested land, that those of Ledwidge's limbs which they could salvage were re-buried in grave Number 5, Row B, the Second plot, Artillery Wood Cemetery. In one of his very last poems, written in a lull in the bombardment, after hearing a robin suddenly sing, he wrote:

This is the song a robin sang
This morning on a broken tree,
It was about the little fields
That call across the world to me.

That night, in the Meath town of Navan, encircled by such little fields, Ledwidge's best friend, Matty McGoona, looked up at the printing works where he was finishing his shift. He later claimed that through the window he caught a passing glimpse of Ledwidge in uniform, calm-looking and full of life. Thinking his friend had been granted leave, McGoona ran out, only to be confronted by an empty street. News reached Meath next day that Ledwidge was dead. His brother Joe was devastated and, in some ways, remained so for the remaining sixty-five years of his life. Their sister Mary came home to comfort their mother in the cottage. Alone in the kitchen, she looked up and also claimed to see Ledwidge there, leaning over her, placing a hand on her shoulder.

He was to haunt his family, haunt his friends and haunt Irish literature in the decades to come.

*

One night recently I returned to Finglas to sit on that mile-stone on the North Road, which somehow still miraculously survives amid all the new developments, with Polish and Romanian now spoken in the new apartment blocks in the spaces where I walked as a boy. Looking back, I knew that, at sixteen, I concocted connections between us that (like all coincidences) were bogus and tenuous. Ledwidge died forty-two years before I was born. He had no say in how I used his life to draw encouragement as a teenager. As a child, I was nobody of consequence until I became somebody in my mind when I wrote my first poem and found a context to encompass my difference: I wasn't an oddball, I was a poet. Poetry provided me with a persona to emerge from the cocoon of shyness. Although Slane and Finglas bore little comparison, Ledwidge was the poet I turned to for inspiration. The night when he sat on that Finglas milestone during his long walk to Slane, he knew that he was throwing away the prospect of a better life and inviting ridicule by returning home. Nothing awaited him except his mother's disappointment when Joe found him huddled behind the shed at dawn, too ashamed to knock, bringing home only a few scribbled lines of verse.

One night, at eighteen, I got drinking with a fellow school leaver. We sat up all night talking in the earnest way of the young. I told him about Francis Ledwidge's life and he was silent for a few moments and then confided a secret – he wanted to be a soldier. He wanted to see different parts of the world and learn skills that he felt the Irish army could not give him. He had therefore decided to enlist in the British army. He was confiding a dangerous secret in 1970s Ireland, with daily murders and bombings in the North. If he let his intentions be widely known in Finglas, he could be beaten up. Even in his absence his parents' house might be attacked. And if he did return to see his family, there was the risk of being kidnapped by the IRA. It was several years before I saw him again, risking a visit home. He was his old self, discussing books and rock music. Only one thing was different – he didn't always hear what I said, being deaf in one ear after the IRA blew up the army coach that he was travelling on in an attempt to murder everyone on board.

In that climate, even Francis Ledwidge's name could provoke an argument. The copy of Curtayne's biography in one library near me was covered in graffiti – Republican readers having doctored the text to scribble slogans on the margins. Yet his poems still survived, with the most unlikely people able to quote lines that were often the only poetry they knew. Part of his fascination, of course, was that he had died young. He was the James Dean of Irish writing. The secret of Marilyn Monroe's mystique is that she never wound up advertising support bras for mature women on television. Buddy Holly never wound up providing paid testimonials to the life-improving wonders of Viagra. The riddle of Ledwidge was partly to do with our ache of never knowing what he would have achieved had he lived. Padraic Colum was an equally gifted young poet who befriended both Ledwidge and Joyce. Colum lived a long and contented life, married, had children, lectured in America and became a distinguished old man of Irish poetry. We saw the full graph of his life, yet today Colum is largely forgotten. With Ledwidge we saw just the tip of the iceberg and ever since then our imaginations have been at play, imagining the rest.

As a boy I swore that one day I would make that pilgrimage to Slane and when I was twenty I finally did. I had intended walking every step, but my survival instincts took over and I thumbed a lift instead. The Pope was visiting Ireland in that autumn of 1979. Most people in Slane seemed preoccupied with discussing the creation of a banner welcoming *El Papa* in case his helicopter flew overhead. But of more immediate concern to some residents along a twilit stretch of country road, leading to where Ledwidge once lived, was the longhaired young stranger pausing to peer at each house. One concerned resident phoned the police barracks because, shortly after starting my quest to see if Ledwidge's cottage still existed, I found myself pinned against a squad car by the local sergeant, who questioned me roughly on the presumption of being a burglar. After I convinced him of my bona fides as a literary pilgrim in search of Ledwidge's old home, the interrogating sergeant became highly convivial and directed me on towards an unmarked and semi-derelict cottage half a mile further along the road.

Dusk had fallen before I reached this abandoned cottage. I couldn't be sure, even from the description in Curtayne's biography, if I had the right place. There was no plaque or landmark. Needing to be certain that this was the cottage where Ledwidge had arrived home after his long walk as a boy, I eventually called to the house next door. A remarkable man, the artist Liam O'Brion, answered my knock. He told me that there was talk of the cottage being knocked down, but some local people were hoping to band together to purchase it as a museum in memory of Ledwidge, with, ironically, my police inquisitor being prominent among them, as were relatives of Ellie Vaughey.

Ledwidge's brother, Joe, was still alive then. The painter urged me to visit him, saying that he welcomed callers but sometimes still got upset when talking about Frank. I stood outside Joe Ledwidge's door in Slane village but couldn't find the courage to knock. Instead I took up Liam O'Brion's offer of a mattress in his studio overlooking Ledwidge's overgrown garden. I sat up all night, surrounded by vivid canvases, staring out at the garden where Ledwidge surely sought refuge from some of the terrible tragedies in that cottage. I was a pilgrim paying my dues, and that night I wondered if one day I would go further and find Ledwidge's actual grave.

At that time it seemed unlikely but, if you live long enough (as Ledwidge never discovered), improbable things do occur. The spot where that stray shell killed Ledwidge is today a quiet field in Flanders, looking far more like the Slane that Ledwidge left behind than the landscape of mud where he died. But in 1998, on the eighty-first anniversary of his death, with nearby potato fields ready for harvesting and black and white cows lazily swishing their tails, the quiet country road adjoining that field, which leads to the nearby village of Boezinge, was thronged with local people and an Irish tricolour finally flew over Flanders.

The locals who came that day knew little about Ledwidge, but each year people around Ieper try to comprehend the endless rows of white crosses surrounding them by focusing on the life of a single individual from either side who lies buried nearby. That evening in 1998 my own personal pilgrimage, which began at a milestone in Finglas at sixteen, ended with the unveiling of a monument in Flanders. A second Irish tricolour – the same flag that McDonagh and others had raised over the General Post Office in 1916 – covered a monument built to mark the exact spot where Ledwidge fell.

Although it was the Flemish authorities and not his own government who were honouring him, Joseph Ledwidge – the son of his faithful brother Joe – and myself were jointly invited to unveil a simple yet highly evocative monument commissioned by the In Flanders Fields Museum, which consists of a portrait of Ledwidge on glass over Ieper brick. The complete text of his poem 'Soliloquy' is printed on the glass in both English and Dutch, with Ledwidge's censored final line restored. Standing there, I thought of his lines from 'At Currabwee': 'For am I not of those who reared/The banner of old Ireland high,/From Dublin town to Turkey's shores…' Although the Irish government played no part in that day, seven years later, on 6 June 2005, the President of Ireland, Mary McAleese (en route to the Island of Ireland Peace Park), visited this monument and Ledwidge's grave, accompanied by the director of the In Flanders Fields Museum, Piet Chielens.

Poems can live on and resurface in surprising ways. This was never more so than when the son of one of Ledwidge's former army comrades visited Artillery Wood Cemetery in the mid-1990s and inscribed by hand the text of Ledwidge's poem 'Crocknaharna' into the visitors' book there. That monument at Boezinge would never have been built had Ledwidge not given his father a copy of the poem while they were together in the trenches, a copy which his father treasured all his life. This poem written into the visitors book was signed 'F.E. Ledwidge' and the cemetery caretaker recognised this name as being on one of the tombstones he tended. The discovery of this hand-written poem led to Piet Chielens in Ieper doing research to discover who exactly this unknown soldier-poet was and then painstakingly locating the exact spot of Ledwidge's death.

After that unveiling of the Ledwidge monument in 1998, people crammed into a school hall in Boezinge where a Ledwidge voice was heard again in Flanders when Joe Ledwidge was coaxed onto the stage. Local people had heard lectures about Ledwidge, but his nephew bridged any language barriers with a mesmerising piece of singing that seemed to bring the ghost of the poet into the room. Links were formed between the villages of his birth and death, with a replica of the Flanders monument unveiled in the garden of Ledwidge's cottage in Slane in 2001, after being constructed by Conrad de Muelenaere and Jean Luc Tillie from Belgium.

Francis Ledwidge was one of thousands of young men from dozen of nationalities who dug trenches, prayed for survival, dreamed of home and eventually died in that

Flanders quagmire. Ledwidge's working life was similar to thousands who died on both sides amid the horrifying stupidity of that war. He never got to live by his poems, though he lived for them. He lived by his hands, as a farm labourer, copper-miner, road-worker and soldier. His second book, *Songs of Peace*, was being printed when he was killed. Dunsany made the selection for a third volume, *Last Songs*, then gathered all three together for a *Collected Poems* that was long out of print, with his uncollected poems in danger of being lost, when Alice Curtayne began her labour of love by collecting together his work for a *Complete Poems* in 1974. In addition to the *Selected Poems* which I edited and Seamus Heaney introduced in 1992, Liam O'Meara has since researched and edited a number of compilations of Ledwidge material, including some prose.

Death was something Ledwidge understood. On one of his last trips home from the war he heard about the death from TB of a young neighbouring boy, Jack Tiernan, whom he used to meet herding cattle for local farmers at dawn, a job he himself had once done. It is typical that from such a tragedy Ledwidge minted a poem of freshness and light. If 'Thomas McDonagh' can also be read as a lament for the adult Ledwidge himself, then his poem for Jack Tiernan might be an epitaph for the younger Ledwidge, rushing with his brother after school to join their mother stooping at work in the frosty dusk of other men's fields, walking home together through the dark listening to her stories, with the gift of poetry already forming in his head.

> He will not come and still I wait.
> He whistles at another gate
> Where angels listen. Ah, I know
> He will not come, yet if I go
> How shall I know he did not pass
> Barefooted in the flowery grass...

The world is calling. I must go.
How shall I know he did not pass
Barefooted in the shining grass?

His cottage in Slane is now open as a museum. The
hungry child who passed through its doors to work in the
fields could never have dreamed that his native village would
today be known as 'Ledwidge Country'. Long after many of
the more famous writers of his time have ceased to be read,
people still recite the poems that, for much of his life, were
the only possessions he truly owned. Francis Ledwidge lived
by his labouring hands and died for an Ireland that was slow
to acknowledge this fact. His death was a monstrous waste,
as were the deaths of the young men from different nations
whose names can barely be accommodated on the huge Ieper
monuments that list the unaccounted dead.

If Ledwidge is remembered because of the enduring
brilliance of several short lyrics, the other men alongside him
in that working party who were all killed by the same shell
are never mentioned. All are buried near him in Artillery
Wood Cemetery. Like Ledwidge, they belonged to the Royal
Inniskilling Fusiliers. They were Private H.P. Evans; Lance
Sergeant J. Harte; Private Frank Mattingley, aged twenty-
nine, son of Walter Francis and Constance Mattingley, of
Witley, Surrey, and husband of Beatrice Ethel Valentine
(formerly Mattingley), of Dorking; Private R. Sharman,
whose remains were unidentifiable but may possibly occupy
the grave with no name next to Ledwidge; and Private
Henry William Newman, aged twenty-three, son of John
and Florence Elizabeth Newman, of Bromley, Kent and
husband of Florence Agnes Gorman (formerly Newman), of
St. Helens, Lancs.

On the same day that Ledwidge died, the Welsh poet
'Hedd Wynn' Ellis Humphrey Evans – who shared a similar
farming background to Ledwidge – was among the eleven

thousand soldiers killed in that same battle. Evans is also buried in the same small cemetery as Ledwidge. But the graves of thousands of young soldiers remain unmarked. Every time a road is built in Ieper or foundations sunk for a house or supermarket, more bodies are churned up by builders, more autopsies held, more clues left for Piet Chielens and others at the In Flanders Fields Museum to piece together, using buttons and fragments of bone to try to identify the missing. Young men like that small crew of road-builders blown to pieces by a random shell on that day in 1917, when men paused at their work to drink scalding tea and turned their thoughts to home, to the secret places in their hearts to which they would never return.